GOODSON MUMBA

In the Executive's Chair

Navigating Corporate Challenges

First edition

ISBN: 9798333619501

This book was professionally typeset on Reedsy.
Find out more at reedsy.com

Contents

Preface

In the modern business landscape, the role of an executive is both demanding and dynamic. The complexity of leading a successful organization requires a strategic vision, financial acumen, and an unwavering commitment to cultivating a positive corporate culture. "In the Executive's Chair: Navigating Corporate Challenges" serves as a comprehensive guide designed to equip current and aspiring executives with the insights, skills, and tools necessary for excelling in this high-stakes environment.

This book addresses the multifaceted aspects of executive leadership, offering practical advice and actionable strategies across fifteen critical areas. Each chapter provides a deep dive into the essentials of effective leadership, from understanding core executive responsibilities to mastering financial management, strategic planning, and leading through change.

Emphasizing the importance of personal development and work-life balance, the book highlights how professional success is intricately linked to personal well-being. Prioritizing continuous learning, building high-performing teams, and fostering a culture of innovation are crucial elements for driving organizations to new heights while ensuring growth and fulfillment.

The journey of an executive involves building strong networks, seeking mentorship, and engaging with stakeholders to achieve organizational success. Real-life examples, case studies, and practical tips are included to provide a roadmap for navigating the complexities of corporate governance, risk management, and global leadership.

"In the Executive's Chair" is not merely a guide for overcoming challenges; it is a blueprint for building a legacy of excellence and integrity. Whether a seasoned executive or an emerging leader, this book serves as a valuable resource, offering insights and inspiration to steer organizations through the turbulent waters of the corporate world.

The aim of this book is to explore the strategies and principles that drive successful executive leadership, providing the tools needed to thrive in an executive role. The challenges and opportunities presented in the following pages are designed to help executives lead with purpose and impact.

Welcome to "In the Executive's Chair: Navigating Corporate Challenges."

Warm regards,

Goodson Mumba

Acknowledgement

I would like to eternally and gratefully acknowledge the Almighty God for the infinite intelligence from His universal mind where we draw from all that we come to know and are yet to know. May I also acknowledge and thank everyone that has played a part in my journey of life in terms of spiritual, moral, emotional and material support.

Dedication

I extend my sincerest gratitude to my beloved wife, Edith Mumba, and our children, Angelina, Lubuto, Letticia, Lulumbi, and Butusho, for their unwavering support and understanding throughout the conception, writing, and eventual publication of this book, despite the sacrifices and challenges they endured.

Disclaimer

This book is a work of fiction. Names, characters, businesses, places, events, and incidents are either the products of the author's imagination or used in a fictitious manner. Any resemblance to actual persons, living or dead, or actual events is purely coincidental.

1

Chapter 1: Understanding the Executive Role

Defining Executive Leadership

Jim Cartwright strode into the boardroom of Cartwright Industries with a sense of purpose, his footsteps echoing off the polished marble floors. The room was a modern marvel, dominated by a long, sleek table and a panoramic view of the city skyline. Yet, despite the impressive surroundings, the atmosphere was thick with skepticism. He could feel the weight of every gaze upon him, questioning his right to lead.

As he took his seat at the head of the table, Jim glanced around at the assembled faces. There was Richard Shaw, his father's old rival, whose smirk barely concealed his disdain. Next to him sat Diane Matthews, the CFO, known for her sharp mind and sharper tongue. On the other side was Paul Bennett, the seasoned COO, a man who had seen the company through numerous challenges. Each of them, in their own way, represented the doubts and expectations Jim had to overcome.

Jim cleared his throat, steeling himself. "Thank you all for being here," he began, his voice firm. "Today, I want to talk about what it means to be an executive leader. For too long, our company has operated on the principles set forth by my father. While those principles served us well, the world has changed, and so must we."

He paused, gauging the room. Richard's smirk widened, as if daring him to say something profound. Diane raised an eyebrow, her pen poised over her notebook. Paul leaned back, arms crossed, waiting.

"Executive leadership," Jim continued, "is not just about making decisions from an ivory tower. It's about setting a vision that inspires, creating a culture that fosters innovation, and leading by example. It's about being accountable, not just to the board or the shareholders, but to every employee who looks to us for guidance."

Jim clicked a button on his laptop, projecting a slide onto the screen. It displayed a simple, yet powerful phrase: **Leadership is Influence**. He turned back to the room, his eyes scanning the faces. "Influence is the core of leadership. It's the ability to inspire action, to drive change, and to create a sense of purpose. Our employees need to believe in our vision and trust in our decisions."

Richard leaned forward, his smirk replaced by a look of challenge. "And what, exactly, is your vision, Jim? What makes you think you can lead this company better than your father did?"

Jim met Richard's gaze without flinching. "My vision is to transform Cartwright Industries into a leader in sustainable manufacturing. To innovate in ways that not only improve our bottom line but also make a positive impact on the world. We need to invest in green technologies, embrace digital transformation, and build a culture of continuous improvement."

Diane nodded slightly, jotting down notes. Paul uncrossed his arms, leaning in with interest. Jim felt a surge of confidence. "Leadership is also about empathy and understanding. It's about knowing the challenges our employees face and working to remove obstacles. It's about being approachable and transparent, creating an environment where ideas can flow freely."

He clicked to the next slide, showing images of the company's various departments and their teams. "I've spent the last few months meeting with employees at all levels. I've listened to their concerns, their ideas, and their aspirations. What I've learned is that we have incredible potential within this company. It's my job to unlock that potential."

Jim's voice grew more passionate. "I'm not here to dictate from above. I'm here to lead alongside you. To make decisions that reflect our collective wisdom. To take risks that drive us forward. And to build a legacy that we can all be proud of."

The room was silent for a moment, the weight of Jim's words sinking in. Then, slowly, Paul began to nod. "I like what I'm hearing," he said. "We need a fresh perspective. And if you're committed to this vision, you'll have my support."

Diane glanced at Richard, who remained silent, his expression unreadable. She turned back to Jim. "It's ambitious," she said. "But I agree with Paul. It's time for change."

Jim allowed himself a small smile. It was just the beginning, but it was a start. "Thank you," he said. "I look forward to working with all of you to make this vision a reality."

As the meeting adjourned, Jim felt a renewed sense of

purpose. Defining executive leadership was more than just words—it was action, commitment, and the unwavering belief in a better future for Cartwright Industries. And he was ready to lead the way.

Responsibilities and Expectations

The boardroom was quiet as the initial meeting concluded. Jim Cartwright gathered his notes, his mind buzzing with the response he had received. Paul's support was a significant win, and Diane's cautious optimism was a good sign. Richard Shaw's silence, however, loomed over him like a storm cloud.

Jim stepped out of the boardroom and into his office, a spacious yet unpretentious room filled with mementos of his father's legacy. Photos of ground-breaking ceremonies, awards, and letters of appreciation lined the walls. As he sat at his desk, Jim's assistant, Claire, knocked lightly on the door.

"Mr. Cartwright, the team is ready for your next meeting," she said with a reassuring smile.

Jim nodded, taking a deep breath. "Thanks, Claire. I'll be right there."

The next meeting was with his senior management team. As he walked into the conference room, the air was charged with a mix of anticipation and apprehension. The room was filled with department heads, all looking to Jim for direction.

"Good afternoon, everyone," Jim began, taking his place at the head of the table. "I want to continue our discussion from this morning about defining executive leadership. We need to address our responsibilities and the expectations placed upon us as leaders."

He paused, looking around the room at the faces of those

who would help him navigate the company through its next chapter. "Our responsibilities as executives are multifaceted. We are the stewards of this company's vision and mission. It's our duty to set clear objectives and to ensure that every team member understands their role in achieving these goals."

Jim clicked the remote, bringing up a slide that outlined key responsibilities: strategic planning, financial oversight, talent management, operational efficiency, and stakeholder engagement.

"Firstly, strategic planning," he said, pointing to the slide. "We must develop strategies that not only address our current challenges but also position us for future growth. This means being proactive, not reactive, and always staying ahead of industry trends."

Next, Jim highlighted financial oversight. "We are accountable for the financial health of Cartwright Industries. This involves careful budgeting, forecasting, and ensuring that every dollar spent is aligned with our strategic objectives. We must be vigilant and transparent, maintaining the trust of our investors and stakeholders."

He moved on to talent management. "Our people are our greatest asset. It's our responsibility to attract, develop, and retain top talent. This means creating an environment where employees feel valued, heard, and motivated to contribute their best work."

Jim glanced at the team, noting their attentive expressions. "Operational efficiency is another critical area. We need to streamline our processes, eliminate waste, and leverage technology to improve productivity. This not only boosts our bottom line but also enhances our competitive edge."

Finally, he touched on stakeholder engagement. "We are

the face of Cartwright Industries to the world. This includes our customers, suppliers, community, and shareholders. We must communicate effectively, act ethically, and build strong, positive relationships."

Jim could see nods of agreement around the table. He pressed on. "In addition to these responsibilities, there are high expectations placed upon us. Our employees look to us for leadership and stability. They expect us to make decisions that are in the best interest of the company and its people. We must lead with integrity, transparency, and a commitment to our values."

He took a deep breath, feeling the weight of his words. "Expectations are also about delivering results. We must set ambitious but achievable goals and hold ourselves accountable for meeting them. This means measuring our performance, learning from our mistakes, and continuously striving for improvement."

Paul Bennett, the COO, leaned forward. "Jim, what are your immediate priorities for us to tackle these responsibilities and meet these expectations?"

Jim appreciated Paul's directness. "Our immediate priorities are to stabilize our finances, launch our new product line, and implement our digital transformation strategy. These initiatives will require all of us to work collaboratively and efficiently."

Diane Matthews, the CFO, spoke up. "I agree with the priorities, Jim. However, we need to ensure that we have the right metrics in place to track our progress and make data-driven decisions."

Jim nodded. "Absolutely, Diane. We'll develop a comprehensive set of KPIs to monitor our performance across all key areas. This will help us stay on track and make informed adjustments as needed."

The meeting continued with a detailed discussion of the specific actions required to achieve their goals. Jim felt a sense of solidarity building among his team. They were beginning to understand not just their roles, but the collective effort needed to navigate the corporate challenges ahead.

As the meeting concluded, Jim felt a renewed sense of purpose. He knew the path forward would be difficult, but with a clear understanding of their responsibilities and the high expectations they had to meet, he felt confident in their ability to lead Cartwright Industries into a prosperous future.

Key Skills and Competencies

Jim Cartwright left the senior management meeting feeling a sense of momentum. The path ahead was daunting, but the team's engagement had been palpable. He knew, however, that to truly steer Cartwright Industries toward success, he needed to ensure that every executive, including himself, possessed the key skills and competencies required for effective leadership.

Returning to his office, Jim found himself drawn to the large window overlooking the bustling city below. He reflected on the qualities that had made his father a respected leader, but he also acknowledged the new demands of today's business environment. His thoughts were interrupted by a knock on the door.

"Jim, the leadership development workshop is ready in the main conference room," Claire informed him.

"Thanks, Claire. I'll be there in a minute," Jim replied,

collecting his thoughts and his materials for the session.

The conference room was set up in a more informal arrangement, conducive to interactive discussions. The senior management team was already assembled, along with a few rising stars from various departments who showed potential for future leadership roles.

Jim started the workshop with a smile. "Good afternoon, everyone. Today, we're going to delve into the key skills and competencies that are crucial for us as executive leaders. Understanding these will not only help us in our current roles but also prepare us for the challenges ahead."

He clicked the remote to display the first slide: **1. Strategic Thinking**. "Strategic thinking is the ability to envision long-term goals and plan accordingly. It's about seeing the big picture and understanding how different elements of the business interconnect. We need to be able to anticipate market trends, evaluate risks, and make decisions that will keep us ahead of the curve."

Jim turned to Diane Matthews. "Diane, could you share an example of strategic thinking from your experience?"

Diane nodded. "Certainly. Last year, we identified a shift in consumer preferences toward more sustainable products. By reallocating resources and investing in eco-friendly materials, we not only met new market demands but also positioned ourselves as leaders in sustainability."

Jim smiled. "Excellent example. Next, let's talk about **2. Communication Skills**. Effective communication is vital for conveying our vision, aligning teams, and building relationships. It's not just about speaking, but also listening and understanding the perspectives of others."

He noticed Paul Bennett's hand raised. "Paul?"

"Jim, I think one of our biggest communication challenges is ensuring that our message is consistent across all levels of the organization. What strategies can we implement to improve this?"

Jim appreciated Paul's insight. "Great point, Paul. We need to establish clear communication channels and regular updates. Town hall meetings, transparent emails, and an open-door policy can foster better communication. It's also important to encourage feedback and make sure everyone feels heard."

The next slide highlighted **3. Emotional Intelligence**. "Emotional intelligence is the ability to manage our own emotions and understand the emotions of others. It helps us build strong relationships, resolve conflicts, and create a positive work environment. This skill is crucial for leadership because it influences how we interact with our teams and make decisions."

Jim shared a personal anecdote. "When I first took over as CEO, I was so focused on results that I overlooked the emotional well-being of our employees. It wasn't until I took the time to listen to their concerns and empathize with their situations that I saw a real improvement in morale and productivity."

The following slide read **4. Decision-Making**. "Decision-making involves choosing the best course of action from multiple options. It requires critical thinking, weighing pros and cons, and being decisive even under pressure. We need to be able to make informed decisions quickly and confidently."

Diane interjected, "Jim, decision-making can be particularly challenging in times of uncertainty. How do you balance data-driven decisions with intuition?"

Jim considered her question. "It's a delicate balance, Diane. Data provides us with valuable insights, but intuition, shaped by experience, is equally important. Combining both allows us to make well-rounded decisions. We should always seek input from our teams and consider diverse perspectives before finalizing any major decisions."

The next key competency appeared on the screen: **5. Adaptability**. "In today's fast-paced world, adaptability is essential. We must be able to pivot when necessary, embrace change, and lead our teams through transitions. This flexibility will help us navigate disruptions and seize new opportunities."

Jim looked around the room, seeing nods of agreement. "Finally, **6. Leadership and People Management**. This encompasses mentoring, motivating, and developing our teams. It's about leading by example, setting clear expectations, and providing the support and resources needed for success."

He paused, letting the significance of these skills sink in. "These competencies are not just boxes to check. They are integral to how we lead and drive our company forward. As we develop these skills in ourselves and our teams, we will be better equipped to face the challenges ahead."

The workshop concluded with an interactive session where team members shared their experiences and strategies for developing these competencies. Jim felt a sense of unity and determination in the room. As they wrapped up, he knew that they were not just discussing abstract concepts, but laying the foundation for the future of Cartwright Industries.

Jim left the conference room feeling invigorated. The journey ahead would require every ounce of their combined skills and competencies, but with a clear understanding and commitment to growth, he was confident they could navigate the corporate challenges and emerge stronger than ever.

Executive vs. Managerial Roles

Jim Cartwright leaned back in his office chair, the late afternoon sun casting long shadows across his desk. The workshop on key skills and competencies had gone well, but he knew the next topic was crucial for aligning his team's understanding of their roles. It was time to address the differences between executive and managerial responsibilities.

Jim decided to approach this topic in a more informal setting to encourage open discussion. He invited his senior management team to a casual dinner at a nearby restaurant, one known for its relaxed atmosphere and excellent food. As they gathered around a large, round table, the mood was congenial, a welcome shift from the tension of the boardroom.

Once everyone had settled and the initial pleasantries were exchanged, Jim cleared his throat to get their attention. "I appreciate all of you taking the time to join me tonight. I wanted to continue our discussion from earlier today by exploring the distinction between executive and managerial roles. Understanding this difference is vital for our collective success."

He paused as the waiter brought out appetizers, then continued. "Executives and managers both play crucial roles within an organization, but their focuses and responsibilities differ significantly. Let's start with executives."

Jim picked up a breadstick and gestured with it, drawing a few chuckles. "As executives, our primary role is to set the strategic direction of the company. We are responsible for envisioning the future, defining long-term goals, and making high-stakes decisions that will guide the organization toward its objectives. Our focus is on the bigger picture, the overall health and growth of the company."

Diane Matthews, the CFO, nodded thoughtfully. "So, it's about setting the vision and ensuring we have the right strategies in place to achieve it."

"Exactly," Jim agreed. "We're also tasked with managing external relationships, such as those with investors, board members, and key stakeholders. Our role involves a lot of forward-thinking and risk management. We need to be aware of industry trends, economic shifts, and emerging opportunities."

Paul Bennett, the COO, interjected, "And how does that differ from what our managers do?"

Jim smiled, glad for the segue. "Managers, on the other hand, are more focused on the operational side of things. They implement the strategies we devise, oversee day-to-day operations, and ensure that their teams meet specific targets and deadlines. Their role is about execution, maintaining efficiency, and addressing immediate issues that arise within their departments."

He leaned forward, emphasizing his next point. "While managers deal with the here and now, ensuring that current processes run smoothly, we as executives must keep our eyes on the horizon, anticipating changes and positioning the company for future success. Both roles are essential, but they require different skill sets and mindsets."

Jim could see the gears turning in their minds, so he continued. "Think of it like this: managers are the hands of the company, executing tasks and making sure everything runs like clockwork. Executives are the eyes and the brain, looking ahead and making strategic decisions. Both are necessary for the body—the company—to function properly."

Diane raised her glass. "So, while managers are managing the present, executives are shaping the future."

Jim nodded, raising his own glass in return. "Well said, Diane. That's precisely it. And understanding this distinction is crucial because it helps us avoid micromanagement and empowers our managers to do their jobs effectively."

He noticed Richard Shaw, usually quiet in these settings, contemplating. Jim decided to address him directly. "Richard, you've seen the company from both a managerial and an executive perspective. What's your take on this distinction?"

Richard looked up, a slight smile playing on his lips. "I've always believed that one of our strengths lies in the ability to distinguish between these roles. When I was in a managerial position, my focus was on optimizing processes and ensuring my team met their goals. As an executive, I've had to broaden my view, considering long-term implications and broader market trends. It's a different kind of challenge, but equally important."

Jim was pleased with Richard's input, sensing a rare moment of alignment. "Thank you, Richard. It's essential for us to respect these roles and not overstep our boundaries. When we, as executives, get too involved in managerial tasks, we lose sight of the strategic vision. Conversely, when managers try to take on strategic roles without the broader context, it can lead to misalignment and inefficiencies."

The main courses arrived, and the conversation shifted to lighter topics. However, Jim felt confident that the message had been conveyed. They were beginning to see the importance of their distinct roles and the necessity of working together harmoniously.

As the dinner wound down, Jim raised his glass once more. "To our continued success and to understanding our roles better. Let's lead with vision, empower our managers, and guide Cartwright Industries to a prosperous future."

Glasses clinked around the table, a sense of camaraderie and shared purpose taking root. Jim knew that this clarity in their roles would be instrumental in navigating the challenges ahead, and he was more determined than ever to lead them toward success.

The Path to Executive Leadership

The dinner had been a success, but Jim Cartwright knew there was more ground to cover. As the team departed, he asked them to reconvene in the boardroom the next morning for a final session on understanding executive roles. This time, he planned to delve into the path to executive leadership.

The following morning, the boardroom was bathed in natural light, creating a welcoming atmosphere. Jim stood at the head of the table, a series of slides ready on the screen behind him. His team settled in, the air filled with a mix of anticipation and curiosity.

"Good morning, everyone," Jim began, his voice confident and clear. "Today, I want to talk about the path to executive leadership. Each of us has taken different routes to get here, and understanding these paths can provide valuable insights for our own growth and for mentoring future leaders within our company."

He clicked to the first slide, which displayed a simple, yet powerful statement: **Executive Leadership: A Journey, Not a Destination**.

Jim turned to his team. "Becoming an executive isn't just about reaching a position. It's about the journey, the experiences, and the growth along the way. I'd like to share some of my journey, and I hope you'll share yours as well."

He clicked to the next slide, which showed a timeline of his career. "I started in the manufacturing department, working on the floor. My father insisted I learn the business from the ground up. It wasn't glamorous, but it taught me the importance of every role in the company."

Paul Bennett, the COO, nodded. "I remember those days, Jim. You were always willing to get your hands dirty and understand the processes."

Jim smiled. "Exactly, Paul. That hands-on experience was invaluable. From there, I moved into a managerial role in logistics. It was my first taste of leadership, and I quickly learned that managing people required a different skill set than managing tasks."

He advanced the slide, showing a photo of a younger Jim leading a team meeting. "As I took on more responsibilities, I faced challenges that forced me to develop my strategic thinking and decision-making skills. One of the toughest lessons was learning to balance empathy with accountability."

Diane Matthews, the CFO, chimed in. "That's a crucial balance, Jim. You need to care about your people, but also hold them to high standards."

"Absolutely," Jim agreed. "And as I progressed, I sought out mentors who could provide guidance and perspective. My father was one, of course, but I also learned from others both inside and outside the company. Their advice helped me navigate complex situations and avoid some pitfalls."

He clicked to the next slide, which highlighted key milestones in his path to becoming CEO. "Each step along the way, I focused on building core competencies—strategic thinking, communication, emotional intelligence, decision-making, and adaptability. These are the skills we discussed yesterday, and they are crucial for anyone aspiring to executive leadership."

Richard Shaw, usually reserved, leaned forward. "Jim, what do you think is the most important trait for someone aspiring to become an executive?"

Jim considered the question carefully. "In my experience, the most important trait is resilience. The path to executive leadership is filled with setbacks and challenges. It's your ability to persevere, learn from failures, and keep pushing forward that ultimately defines your success."

He looked around the table. "Now, I'd like to hear from you. What were some pivotal moments in your journeys to executive leadership?"

Paul was the first to speak. "For me, it was when I was tasked with turning around an underperforming plant. It required every ounce of my problem-solving skills and tested my leadership. But it taught me the importance of building a strong, motivated team."

Diane nodded. "In my case, it was navigating the financial crisis a decade ago. Keeping the company afloat and making tough decisions under pressure taught me the value of strategic financial management and transparent communication."

Richard Shaw spoke next, surprising everyone. "I started in sales, working my way up through the ranks. The competition was fierce, and I learned early on that building relationships and understanding customer needs were key to success. It wasn't always smooth, but those experiences shaped my approach to leadership."

Jim appreciated Richard's candor. "Thank you all for sharing. Each of our paths is unique, but the common thread is growth through experience. As we continue to lead Cartwright Industries, we must also focus on identifying and nurturing future leaders. Providing them with opportunities to learn, grow, and take on new challenges is essential for our long-term success."

He clicked to the final slide, which displayed the words: **Mentorship, Opportunity, and Continuous Learning**. "These are the pillars of developing executive leaders. Let's commit to fostering an environment where our future leaders can thrive, just as we have."

As the meeting concluded, Jim felt a sense of fulfillment. They had not only deepened their understanding of executive roles but also connected on a personal level, sharing the journeys that brought them to this point. He knew that with this foundation, they could navigate any corporate challenge that lay ahead.

Balancing Authority and Accountability

The team had covered a lot of ground over the past few days, but Jim Cartwright knew there was one more crucial aspect to address before they could move forward with complete clarity: balancing authority and accountability. He decided to take a different approach for this session, inviting a guest speaker to provide an outside perspective.

The next morning, the boardroom was abuzz with curiosity.

Jim stood at the front, ready to introduce their guest. "Good morning, everyone. Today, we're going to discuss the delicate balance of authority and accountability. To help us with this, I've invited Dr. Elaine Roberts, an expert in organizational leadership and ethics."

Dr. Roberts, a distinguished woman with a calm yet commanding presence, smiled warmly as she stood. "Thank you, Jim. It's a pleasure to be here. Balancing authority and accountability is a cornerstone of effective leadership, and I'm excited to share some insights with you today."

She began with a story. "Several years ago, I was consulting for a company that was facing significant internal strife. The executives had plenty of authority but lacked accountability. This led to a toxic culture and plummeting performance. The turning point came when the CEO realized that true leadership meant holding himself and his team accountable for their actions and decisions."

Dr. Roberts turned to the group. "Authority gives you the power to make decisions and direct others. Accountability ensures that you are answerable for the outcomes of those decisions. These two elements must be in balance to maintain trust and effectiveness within an organization."

Jim watched as his team listened intently. He knew they understood the importance of what she was saying, but he wanted to ensure the concepts were fully internalized. "Dr. Roberts, could you provide some practical strategies for balancing authority and accountability?"

"Of course," she replied. "Let's start with transparency. As leaders, you must be open about your decision-making processes and the reasons behind them. This builds trust and helps your team understand that your authority is being exercised responsibly."

Jim nodded. "Transparency has been a key focus for us, especially in our communications. But it's something we need to continually improve."

Dr. Roberts continued, "Next is delegation. Empower your managers by delegating authority, but also hold them accountable for their areas of responsibility. This not only builds their leadership skills but also ensures that accountability is distributed throughout the organization."

Paul Bennett, the COO, raised his hand. "How do we ensure that delegation doesn't lead to abdication of our own responsibilities?"

"Excellent question, Paul," Dr. Roberts said. "Delegation should come with clear expectations and regular check-ins. It's about providing support and oversight without micromanaging. You're still accountable for the overall outcomes, but you trust your managers to handle the details."

Jim saw the importance of this. "We need to find that balance between giving our managers the freedom to lead and ensuring we're all moving in the same direction."

Dr. Roberts smiled. "Exactly, Jim. Another key strategy is fostering a culture of accountability. This means setting clear goals, measuring performance, and addressing issues promptly. Recognize successes and learn from failures. Accountability should be seen as a positive force for growth and improvement."

Diane Matthews, the CFO, spoke up. "We've started implementing more robust performance metrics, but there's still a cultural shift that needs to happen. How do we change the perception of accountability from punitive to developmental?"

Dr. Roberts nodded. "It starts with leadership. Model the behavior you want to see. When mistakes happen, focus on learning and improvement rather than blame. Celebrate achievements and progress. Make accountability part of your leadership values."

Jim felt the room's energy shift as they absorbed these insights. He could see the wheels turning in their minds, and he knew this was a pivotal moment. "Dr. Roberts, your insights have been incredibly valuable. Can you give us one final piece of advice?"

Dr. Roberts paused thoughtfully. "Remember that authority and accountability are two sides of the same coin. Use your authority wisely and always hold yourselves accountable. This balance will earn you the trust and respect of your team, fostering a culture where everyone feels responsible for the success of the organization."

As Dr. Roberts concluded her session, Jim took the floor once more. "Thank you, Dr. Roberts, for your wisdom. Balancing authority and accountability is something we must all commit to as we lead Cartwright Industries. Let's take these lessons to heart and ensure that our actions reflect the balance we seek."

The team applauded, and Jim felt a renewed sense of purpose. The journey to effective executive leadership was ongoing, but with these principles guiding them, he was confident they could navigate any challenge that lay ahead.

Chapter 2: Strategic Vision and Planning

Crafting a Clear Vision

Jim Cartwright stood at the front of the conference room, feeling a sense of anticipation. Today's session was crucial. They had laid the groundwork by understanding their roles, but now it was time to chart the future. The topic was "Crafting a Clear Vision," the foundation of any strategic planning process.

The senior management team settled in, notebooks and tablets at the ready. Jim started with a question to engage them immediately. "What do you think makes a vision compelling and actionable?"

Paul Bennett, the COO, was the first to respond. "A vision should be inspiring, something that motivates everyone in the organization. It should be clear enough that everyone understands where we're headed."

Jim nodded. "Exactly, Paul. A vision needs to be both

aspirational and attainable. It's a guiding star that aligns our efforts and decisions. Today, we're going to define what that star looks like for Cartwright Industries."

He clicked the remote, and a slide appeared with the words: **Crafting a Clear Vision: Inspire, Align, Achieve**.

"Before we dive into crafting our vision, let's look at some examples from companies that have done this successfully." Jim showed slides featuring well-known corporate visions, such as Amazon's "To be Earth's most customer-centric company" and Tesla's "To accelerate the world's transition to sustainable energy."

"These visions are simple, yet powerful," Jim continued. "They provide a clear direction and purpose. Our goal today is to create a vision that does the same for Cartwright Industries."

He then split the team into small groups, each tasked with brainstorming key elements that should be part of their vision. "Think about our strengths, our market position, and where we want to be in the next five to ten years," Jim instructed.

As the groups worked, Jim circulated the room, listening to the discussions. He heard a mix of enthusiasm and pragmatism, which he found encouraging. After twenty minutes, he called everyone back together.

"Let's hear what you've come up with," Jim said, eager to see the results of their brainstorming.

Diane Matthews, the CFO, stood up first. "Our group focused on our commitment to innovation and customer satisfaction. We believe our vision should emphasize our dedication to creating cutting-edge solutions that meet our customers' evolving needs."

Paul followed, adding, "We also discussed the importance of

sustainability. As a manufacturing company, we have a responsibility to minimize our environmental impact. Our vision should reflect our commitment to sustainable practices."

Jim nodded thoughtfully. "Excellent points. Innovation, customer satisfaction, and sustainability are crucial. What else?"

Richard Shaw, the head of sales, spoke up. "We need to highlight our global reach and our aspiration to be a market leader. Our vision should reflect our ambition to expand and dominate in our industry."

Jim smiled. "Great input, Richard. Now, let's synthesize these ideas into a cohesive vision statement."

He moved to a whiteboard and wrote down the key themes: Innovation, Customer Satisfaction, Sustainability, and Global Leadership. "These are the pillars of our vision. How can we combine them into a single, compelling statement?"

The team engaged in a lively discussion, refining their ideas. After some back and forth, they settled on a draft vision statement: "To lead the global manufacturing industry through innovation, sustainability, and unmatched customer satisfaction."

Jim wrote it on the whiteboard, underlining it for emphasis. "This is a great start. It's clear, ambitious, and reflects our core values and goals. Let's take a moment to consider if this resonates with who we are and where we want to go."

He saw nods of agreement around the room. "We'll refine this further, but I believe we're on the right track. A clear vision like this will guide our strategic planning and help us align our efforts. It's something we can all rally behind."

Jim concluded the session with a sense of accomplishment. Crafting a clear vision was only the first step, but it was a critical one. He felt confident that with this foundation, Cartwright Industries was poised to navigate its future with purpose and direction. As the team left the room, he could see a renewed energy and focus in their eyes, a clear sign that they were ready to turn their vision into reality.

Long-term vs. Short-term Goals

With their vision statement freshly crafted, Jim Cartwright knew the next step was to break down their grand aspirations into actionable goals. He gathered his senior management team in the boardroom once more, the atmosphere charged with a sense of purpose.

"Good morning, everyone," Jim began. "Now that we have a clear vision, our task is to translate that vision into both long-term and short-term goals. This will provide us with a roadmap to achieve our aspirations."

He clicked the remote, and the screen displayed the title: **Long-term vs. Short-term Goals: Balancing Immediate Needs with Future Ambitions**.

Jim looked around the room, making eye contact with each member of his team. "Balancing long-term and short-term goals is crucial. We need to ensure that our day-to-day operations support our long-term vision while also addressing immediate challenges."

He walked over to a flipchart and drew two columns labeled "Long-term" and "Short-term". "Let's start by defining what we mean by long-term and short-term goals. Paul, could you share your thoughts on the difference?"

Paul Bennett, the COO, leaned forward. "Long-term goals are those that we aim to achieve in three to five years or even further out. They're strategic and often involve significant changes or growth. Short-term goals, on the other hand, are those we want to achieve in the next year or less. They're more tactical and help us maintain momentum toward our long-term objectives."

Jim nodded. "Exactly. Both types of goals are essential. Long-term goals keep us focused on our vision, while short-term goals provide the steps needed to get there. Let's start with our long-term goals."

He wrote "Long-term" at the top of the first column. "Based on our vision, what are some long-term goals we should aim for?"

Diane Matthews, the CFO, spoke first. "We need to aim for a 30% reduction in our carbon footprint within the next five years. This aligns with our commitment to sustainability."

Jim wrote it down. "Great. What else?"

Richard Shaw, the head of sales, added, "Expanding our market presence in Asia. It's a growing market with significant potential for us. We should set a goal to double our market share there in the next five years."

Jim added this to the list. "Excellent. Any other long-term goals?"

Paul chimed in, "We should also aim to be recognized as a top innovator in our industry. That could involve setting up an innovation lab and increasing our R&D budget by 50% over the next three years."

Jim jotted it down. "Perfect. Now, let's switch to short-term goals. What immediate actions can we take to start moving toward these long-term objectives?"

He moved to the "Short-term" column and wrote the first goal. "For reducing our carbon footprint, a short-term goal could be to conduct an energy audit of all our facilities within the next six months and identify areas for improvement."

Diane nodded. "And we could implement a recycling program across all offices within the next quarter."

Jim wrote that down as well. "Great. For expanding in Asia, a short-term goal might be to establish a partnership with a local distributor by the end of this year."

Richard agreed. "And we could also attend major industry trade shows in Asia within the next six months to increase our visibility."

Jim added these to the list. "For becoming a top innovator, we could start by hiring a new head of R&D and setting up a dedicated innovation team within the next three months."

Paul added, "And we could initiate a company-wide innovation challenge to generate new ideas and foster a culture of innovation."

Jim smiled, writing down the last of the short-term goals. "This is excellent. We've identified concrete steps that we can start taking immediately, which will pave the way for achieving our long-term goals."

He stepped back, looking at the flipchart filled with their collective goals. "Remember, the key to success is regularly reviewing our progress and adjusting our goals as needed. Long-term goals will keep us aligned with our vision, but it's the short-term goals that will build the bridge to get us there."

The team sat back, absorbing the plan. Jim could see the determination in their faces. They were ready to tackle the immediate challenges while keeping an eye on the future.

"Let's commit to these goals and start making our vision a reality," Jim concluded. "Together, we can achieve great things."

As the team dispersed to start implementing their short-term goals, Jim felt a surge of optimism. They had a clear vision and a solid plan. Now, it was time to execute and turn their strategic vision into tangible success.

Strategic Analysis Tools

Jim Cartwright had seen a significant shift in his team's energy since they had crafted their vision and established their goals. Now, it was time to equip them with the tools needed to navigate the complexities of strategic planning. He decided to introduce them to some powerful strategic analysis tools that would help them make informed decisions and stay aligned with their objectives.

The boardroom was set up with a projector and several flipcharts. Jim was eager to demonstrate how these tools could provide insights into their strategic planning process. As his team gathered, he sensed a mix of curiosity and readiness.

"Good morning, everyone," Jim began. "Today, we'll dive into strategic analysis tools that will help us assess our current situation, identify opportunities and threats, and make informed decisions. These tools are essential for guiding our strategic planning and ensuring we stay on course."

He clicked the remote, and the first slide appeared: **Strategic Analysis Tools: SWOT, PESTLE, and Porter's Five Forces**.

"Let's start with the SWOT analysis," Jim said. "SWOT stands for Strengths, Weaknesses, Opportunities, and Threats. It's a simple yet powerful tool for understanding our internal and external environments."

He handed out printed worksheets to each team member

and displayed a blank SWOT matrix on the screen. "I want each of you to think about our company's strengths and weaknesses, as well as the opportunities and threats we face in the market. Let's take ten minutes to fill these out, and then we'll discuss them."

The room fell into focused silence as the team wrote down their thoughts. Jim walked around, glancing at their worksheets, pleased to see insightful reflections.

After ten minutes, Jim called for their attention. "Let's start with strengths. What did you come up with?"

Paul Bennett, the COO, spoke first. "Our advanced manufacturing technology and skilled workforce are definitely strengths. They give us a competitive edge."

Diane Matthews, the CFO, added, "Our strong financial health and diverse product portfolio are also significant strengths."

Jim wrote these on the flipchart under the "Strengths" column. "Great. Now, what about weaknesses?"

Richard Shaw, the head of sales, said, "Our supply chain is still vulnerable to disruptions, as we saw during the pandemic. We need to improve its resilience."

Paul agreed. "Also, our marketing efforts could be more robust. We have great products, but we need to better communicate their value to our customers."

Jim noted these down. "Excellent points. Now, let's move to opportunities. What market trends or changes could we capitalize on?"

Diane suggested, "There's a growing demand for sustainable products. We can develop eco-friendly solutions that appeal to environmentally conscious consumers."

Richard added, "Expanding our digital presence and e-commerce capabilities can open new revenue streams, especially in international markets."

Jim wrote these in the "Opportunities" column. "Finally, what threats do we face?"

Paul responded, "Increasing competition from low-cost manufacturers in Asia. They're putting pressure on our pricing."

Diane added, "Economic uncertainty and fluctuating raw material prices are also significant threats."

Jim completed the SWOT matrix and stepped back. "This gives us a clear picture of where we stand and what we need to focus on. Now, let's look at another tool: PESTLE analysis."

He clicked to the next slide, displaying the PESTLE framework: Political, Economic, Social, Technological, Legal, and Environmental factors. "PESTLE helps us understand the macro-environmental factors that could impact our business. Let's take another ten minutes to consider these factors."

The team got to work again, analyzing how each factor could influence their strategic planning. Once the time was up, Jim facilitated a discussion on their findings.

"Political factors," Jim began. "Any thoughts?"

Diane said, "Changes in trade policies and tariffs could affect our international operations. We need to stay informed and adaptable."

Jim nodded and moved on. "Economic factors?"

Richard replied, "Inflation rates and currency fluctuations can impact our costs and pricing strategies."

"Social factors?" Jim asked.

Paul said, "There's a shift towards more personalized and customer-centric products. We need to adapt our offerings to meet these evolving preferences."

Jim captured their insights on the flipchart. "Technological factors?"

Diane answered, "Advancements in automation and artificial intelligence can enhance our production efficiency and product innovation."

"Legal factors?" Jim continued.

Paul noted, "Compliance with international regulations and standards is critical, especially as we expand globally."

Finally, Jim asked, "Environmental factors?"

Richard said, "We need to focus on sustainability and reducing our environmental footprint to meet regulatory requirements and customer expectations."

Jim completed the PESTLE analysis and addressed the team. "These insights will help us navigate the external environment and make strategic decisions that align with our vision. Now, let's move on to Porter's Five Forces."

He clicked to the next slide, which showed Porter's Five Forces: Competitive Rivalry, Threat of New Entrants, Threat of Substitutes, Bargaining Power of Suppliers, and Bargaining Power of Customers.

"These forces help us understand the competitive dynamics of our industry," Jim explained. "Let's take a few minutes to discuss each force and its impact on our business."

The team engaged in a detailed discussion, analyzing each force and how it influenced their strategic position. Jim captured their insights, emphasizing the importance of understanding these dynamics to stay competitive.

"Competitive rivalry," Jim summarized. "We face strong competition, but our innovation and customer focus can set us apart."

"Threat of new entrants," Paul said. "High, but we can

mitigate it through strong brand loyalty and continuous innovation."

"Threat of substitutes," Diane added. "Moderate, but we need to keep improving our products to maintain our edge."

"Bargaining power of suppliers," Richard noted. "High, due to limited sources for some raw materials. We need to diversify our supply base."

"Bargaining power of customers," Jim concluded. "Moderate. Offering unique value and superior customer service can reduce their power."

As the session wrapped up, Jim felt a sense of accomplishment. They had not only identified their strengths and weaknesses but also gained a deeper understanding of the external factors influencing their strategic decisions.

"These tools provide us with a comprehensive view of our strategic landscape," Jim said. "By regularly using SWOT, PESTLE, and Porter's Five Forces, we can make informed decisions and stay aligned with our vision. Let's commit to integrating these analyses into our strategic planning process."

The team nodded in agreement, ready to leverage these tools to navigate their future. Jim felt confident that with these insights, Cartwright Industries was well-equipped to achieve its strategic goals and realize its vision.

Implementing Effective Plans

With a clear vision, concrete goals, and a thorough understanding of their strategic landscape, Jim Cartwright and his senior management team were now ready to move forward with implementing effective plans. The atmosphere in the boardroom was charged with determination and focus as they convened to tackle the next crucial step.

"Good morning, everyone," Jim began, his voice carrying a note of optimism. "Today, we're going to discuss how we can effectively implement the plans we've developed. Our success hinges not just on our strategies, but on our ability to execute them well."

He clicked the remote, revealing the slide titled **Implementing Effective Plans: From Strategy to Action**.

"Effective implementation requires careful planning, clear communication, and diligent execution," Jim continued. "Let's break this down into actionable steps."

He walked over to the flipchart, where he had outlined the key steps for implementing effective plans:

1. **Setting Clear Objectives and KPIs**
2. **Allocating Resources**
3. **Developing Action Plans**
4. **Establishing Timelines**
5. **Communicating the Plan**
6. **Monitoring and Adjusting**

"First, we need to set clear objectives and Key Performance Indicators (KPIs) for each of our goals," Jim said. "KPIs will help us measure our progress and ensure we stay on track. Let's start with our goal to reduce our carbon footprint."

Diane Matthews, the CFO, spoke up. "One objective could be to decrease energy consumption by 15% within the first year. A KPI for this might be tracking monthly energy usage and comparing it to our baseline data."

Jim wrote this on the flipchart under the first step. "Excellent. What about our goal to expand our market presence in

Asia?"

Paul Bennett, the COO, responded, "An objective could be to increase sales in Asia by 20% in the next year. A KPI might be monthly sales figures by region."

Jim added this to the list. "Great. Next, we need to allocate the necessary resources. This includes budget, personnel, and technology. For our sustainability initiatives, what resources do we need?"

Diane answered, "We'll need to invest in energy-efficient equipment and possibly hire a sustainability consultant to guide us through the process."

Jim wrote this down and moved on. "For expanding in Asia, we'll need additional marketing budget and possibly a new team dedicated to that region."

Richard Shaw, the head of sales, nodded. "We might also need to establish a regional office to better serve our customers there."

"Good points," Jim said, noting them. "Now, let's develop detailed action plans. These plans should outline the specific steps needed to achieve our objectives."

He divided the team into smaller groups, each tasked with drafting action plans for their respective goals. After a focused brainstorming session, the groups presented their plans.

"For reducing energy consumption," Diane's group shared, "we'll conduct an energy audit, upgrade to LED lighting, and implement an employee awareness program on energy-saving practices."

Jim nodded. "Very detailed. For expanding in Asia?"

Paul's group responded, "We'll start with market research to identify key opportunities, develop targeted marketing campaigns, and establish partnerships with local distributors."

"Excellent," Jim said, adding these to the flipchart. "Next, we need to establish timelines. This helps ensure we meet our objectives on schedule. Let's set some realistic deadlines for each step."

Diane suggested, "We can complete the energy audit within three months, start the lighting upgrades in the fourth month, and roll out the awareness program in the fifth month."

Richard added for their goal, "Market research can be done in two months, marketing campaigns launched in the third month, and partnerships established by the sixth month."

Jim recorded the timelines. "Perfect. Now, communication is key to successful implementation. We need to ensure everyone in the organization understands the plan, their role in it, and the timelines."

He outlined a communication plan on the flipchart. "We'll hold company-wide meetings to introduce the plans, send out detailed emails, and create an internal portal where employees can track progress and updates."

Finally, Jim addressed the last step. "Monitoring and adjusting our plans is crucial. We need to regularly review our progress, celebrate successes, and make adjustments as needed."

Paul suggested, "We could set up monthly review meetings to assess our progress against the KPIs and timelines."

Jim agreed. "That's a great idea. These meetings will keep us accountable and allow us to address any issues promptly."

He looked around the room, seeing the confidence in his team's eyes. "By following these steps, we can ensure that our strategic plans are effectively implemented. Let's commit to this process and work together to turn our vision into reality."

The team nodded, ready to embark on the next phase of their

journey. Jim felt a deep sense of satisfaction. They had a clear vision, actionable goals, and a solid plan for implementation. Now, it was time to execute and lead Cartwright Industries toward a future of growth and innovation.

As the meeting adjourned, Jim knew that the real work was just beginning. But with the dedication and commitment of his team, he was confident they would succeed in navigating the corporate challenges ahead.

Aligning Vision with Corporate Culture

Jim Cartwright knew that for their strategic plans to succeed, they needed more than just clear objectives and effective implementation. The company's vision had to resonate deeply within the corporate culture. Without this alignment, even the best-laid plans would struggle to take root. This was the focus of today's meeting.

The senior management team gathered in the company's main conference room, which had large windows overlooking the cityscape. The morning sun cast a warm glow over the room, adding to the sense of optimism and energy.

"Good morning, everyone," Jim began. "Today, we're going to discuss how we can align our vision with our corporate culture. Our culture is the foundation upon which our vision will either thrive or falter. It's crucial that every member of our organization not only understands our vision but feels connected to it."

He clicked the remote, and the slide on the screen read: **Aligning Vision with Corporate Culture: Building a Unified Purpose**.

"Let's start by defining what our current corporate culture

is," Jim said. "How would you describe it?"

Paul Bennett, the COO, leaned forward. "I'd say our culture is innovative but somewhat traditional. We value creativity, but we also have deeply ingrained practices and processes."

Diane Matthews, the CFO, added, "We're results-driven and take pride in our quality and efficiency. However, there's a need for more openness and collaboration."

Jim nodded. "Exactly. We have strong foundations, but we need to evolve. Our vision calls for innovation, sustainability, and global leadership. To achieve this, our culture must embrace these values fully."

He walked over to a whiteboard and wrote down their vision statement: **To lead the global manufacturing industry through innovation, sustainability, and unmatched customer satisfaction.**

"Now, let's break down our vision into cultural values," Jim said. "What values must our culture embody to support this vision?"

Richard Shaw, the head of sales, spoke up. "Innovation. We need a culture that encourages and rewards creative thinking and risk-taking."

Jim wrote "Innovation" on the board. "Absolutely. What else?"

Diane responded, "Sustainability. This needs to be more than just a strategy; it has to be a core value that influences every decision we make."

Jim added "Sustainability" to the list. "Good. And?"

Paul said, "Customer-centricity. We need to prioritize our customers' needs and satisfaction in everything we do."

Jim completed the list with "Customer-centricity". "Great. These are the values that should permeate our corporate culture. Now, how do we make this happen?"

He clicked to the next slide: **Steps to Align Vision with Culture**.

1. **Communicate the Vision and Values**
2. **Embed Values in Everyday Actions**
3. **Leadership by Example**
4. **Reward and Recognition**
5. **Continuous Feedback and Improvement**

"First, we need to communicate our vision and values clearly and consistently," Jim said. "This means more than just emails and meetings. We need to tell a compelling story that resonates with everyone."

Diane suggested, "We could create a series of videos featuring employees from different departments talking about what the vision means to them and how it influences their work."

Jim nodded. "Great idea. Storytelling can be a powerful tool. Next, we need to embed these values in our everyday actions. This means our policies, procedures, and practices must reflect our vision."

Paul added, "We can start by revisiting our onboarding process to ensure new hires understand and align with our values from day one."

"Exactly," Jim said, writing it down. "Leadership by example is crucial. We, as leaders, must embody these values in everything we do."

Richard agreed. "If we're promoting innovation, we need to show that we're willing to take risks and try new things ourselves."

"Right," Jim said. "Next, reward and recognition. We need

to acknowledge and reward behaviors that reflect our values."

Diane suggested, "We could introduce an 'Innovation of the Month' award and a sustainability recognition program."

"Excellent," Jim said, noting it. "Finally, continuous feedback and improvement. We need to create a culture of open communication where employees feel comfortable sharing their ideas and feedback."

Paul proposed, "Regular town hall meetings and anonymous feedback channels could help with this."

Jim wrote the last point down and stepped back. "These steps will help us align our culture with our vision. Remember, this is an ongoing process. We need to be patient and persistent."

He looked around the room, seeing the commitment in his team's faces. "Let's commit to fostering a culture that supports our vision. Together, we can create an environment where our employees are not just working towards a goal but are deeply invested in our collective success."

As the meeting adjourned, Jim felt a renewed sense of purpose. Aligning their vision with the corporate culture would not be easy, but it was essential for their long-term success. He was confident that with the dedication and leadership of his team, they could transform Cartwright Industries into a company where the vision and culture were in perfect harmony.

Monitoring and Adjusting Strategies

Jim Cartwright sat in his corner office, the city's skyline a backdrop to his contemplative mood. The quarterly review meeting was about to begin, and Jim knew this session was crucial. It wasn't just about tracking progress; it was about ensuring their strategies remained aligned with their ever-changing environment.

He took a deep breath, stood up, and walked toward the boardroom where his senior management team was already gathering. As he entered, the room fell silent, a mix of anticipation and readiness in the air.

"Good morning, everyone," Jim began, his voice steady and resolute. "Today, we're going to focus on monitoring and adjusting our strategies. This is a vital part of our role as executives. We need to be agile and responsive to ensure we stay on course toward our goals."

He clicked the remote, and the slide on the screen read: **Monitoring and Adjusting Strategies: Ensuring Continuous Alignment and Improvement**.

"Let's start by reviewing our key performance indicators (KPIs) and the progress we've made towards our goals," Jim said, directing everyone's attention to the first chart. "Paul, could you give us an overview of our operational performance?"

Paul Bennett, the COO, stood up. "Certainly, Jim. Our production efficiency has improved by 10% since implementing the new processes. However, we've encountered some supply chain disruptions that have affected our delivery times."

Jim nodded. "Thank you, Paul. Supply chain disruptions are a significant concern. We need to address these issues promptly. Diane, how are we doing financially?"

Diane Matthews, the CFO, took the floor. "Financially, we're on track. Our revenue has increased by 8%, and we've managed to reduce overhead costs by 5%. However, the fluctuating costs of raw materials are impacting our margins."

Jim made a note. "Good progress overall, but these raw material costs are something we need to monitor closely. Richard, how about our market expansion efforts?"

Richard Shaw, the head of sales, stood up. "We've made headway in Asia, with a 15% increase in market share. However, our marketing campaigns are not as effective as we'd hoped, and we're seeing a lower-than-expected return on investment."

Jim clicked to the next slide, which displayed a summary of the key issues identified: supply chain disruptions, raw material cost fluctuations, and underperforming marketing campaigns.

"These are the areas we need to focus on," Jim said. "Now, let's discuss how we can adjust our strategies to address these challenges."

He turned to Paul. "For the supply chain issues, what steps can we take to mitigate these disruptions?"

Paul responded, "We can diversify our supplier base to reduce dependency on a few key suppliers. Additionally, we should invest in better supply chain management software to enhance our visibility and responsiveness."

Jim nodded. "Excellent suggestions. Diane, how can we better manage the fluctuating costs of raw materials?"

Diane replied, "We should consider entering into long-term contracts with our suppliers to lock in prices. Another option is to explore alternative materials that are less volatile in price."

"Good ideas," Jim said, making notes. "And Richard, what adjustments can we make to improve the effectiveness of our marketing campaigns?"

Richard suggested, "We need to re-evaluate our marketing strategies and possibly shift more focus to digital channels, which can offer better targeting and ROI. Also, we should conduct market research to better understand our customers' preferences and tailor our messages accordingly."

Jim clicked to the final slide, which summarized their adjusted strategies: diversifying suppliers, securing long-term contracts, exploring alternative materials, enhancing digital marketing efforts, and conducting market research.

"These adjustments should help us stay aligned with our goals and address the challenges we're facing," Jim said. "But remember, monitoring and adjusting strategies is an ongoing process. We need to stay vigilant and ready to adapt as new information comes in."

He looked around the room, seeing the determination in his team's faces. "Let's commit to regular reviews and open communication. By continuously monitoring our progress and being willing to adjust our strategies, we can ensure we stay on the path to success."

The team nodded in agreement, ready to tackle the next steps. As the meeting adjourned, Jim felt a renewed sense of confidence. They had a clear plan, and with the dedication and agility of his team, he was certain they could navigate any challenges that came their way.

Back in his office, Jim reflected on the importance of monitoring and adjusting strategies. It was a reminder that in the executive's chair, success wasn't just about having a great plan—it was about continuously steering the ship, responding to the winds of change, and always striving for improvement.

Chapter 3: Building High-Performing Teams

Recruiting Top Talent

Jim Cartwright was well aware that the strength of a company lay in its people. To achieve their ambitious vision, Cartwright Industries needed to build high-performing teams, starting with recruiting top talent. Today, he was set to meet with the HR team to revamp their recruitment strategy.

The conference room was abuzz with discussion when Jim entered. HR Director, Janet Ross, and her team were already there, along with several department heads. Jim took his seat at the head of the table, bringing the room to a focused silence.

"Good morning, everyone," Jim began. "We've done a lot of great work defining our vision and setting our goals, but none of this will matter if we don't have the right people in place to execute our plans. Recruiting top talent is our priority."

Janet nodded. "Absolutely, Jim. We've been reviewing our

current recruitment processes, and it's clear we need to make some significant changes to attract and retain the best talent."

Jim clicked the remote, bringing up the slide titled **Recruiting Top Talent: Strategies for Success**.

"Let's start by identifying what 'top talent' means for us," Jim said. "We need to be clear on the qualities and skills we're looking for in our future employees."

Paul Bennett, the COO, spoke up. "We need people who are not only highly skilled but also align with our values of innovation, sustainability, and customer-centricity."

Jim wrote this on the whiteboard. "Agreed. It's crucial that our new hires not only have the technical abilities but also fit our culture and vision. Janet , how can we ensure our recruitment process reflects this?"

Janet stood up. "We need to start with a more targeted approach in our job descriptions and recruitment channels. We should highlight our company's commitment to innovation and sustainability to attract candidates who share these values."

Jim nodded. "Good point. Job descriptions should be more than just a list of tasks—they should convey our vision and culture."

Diane Matthews, the CFO, added, "We should also leverage our network and employee referrals more effectively. Our current employees know our culture best and can recommend people who would be a good fit."

"Excellent suggestion," Jim said, making a note. "What about the interview process? How can we ensure we're selecting the right candidates?"

Richard Shaw, the head of sales, chimed in. "We should include practical assessments or problem-solving exercises that reflect the challenges they'll face here. This way, we can see how they think and approach real-world problems."

Janet agreed. "And we should incorporate cultural fit interviews. We can have candidates meet with potential peers and other department heads to see if they align with our values and work style."

Jim added this to the list. "These are all great ideas. Now, let's talk about the recruitment channels. Where should we be looking for top talent?"

Janet replied, "We need to diversify our recruitment channels. Beyond traditional job boards, we should look at industry-specific forums, university partnerships, and social media platforms. We should also attend industry conferences and career fairs."

Paul added, "And we should consider working with specialized recruitment agencies that have a track record of finding top talent in our industry."

Jim wrote down their suggestions. "We also need to build our employer brand. Potential candidates should see Cartwright Industries as a great place to work."

Diane suggested, "We can create content showcasing our projects, employee testimonials, and our commitment to professional development and work-life balance. Sharing this on our website and social media can attract top talent."

Jim nodded. "Great idea. We should also highlight our successes and innovations. This will not only attract top talent but also instill pride in our current employees."

He clicked to the final slide, summarizing their strategies: defining key qualities, enhancing job descriptions, leveraging networks and referrals, incorporating practical assessments, diversifying recruitment channels, and building a strong employer brand.

"These strategies will help us attract the top talent we need," Jim said. "Remember, the goal is to find individuals who are not only skilled but also share our vision and values."

He looked around the room, seeing the determination in his team's faces. "Let's implement these changes and start building the high-performing teams that will drive our success."

As the meeting adjourned, Jim felt a renewed sense of optimism. With a clear strategy for recruiting top talent, he was confident that Cartwright Industries was on the path to attracting and retaining the best people. This, he knew, was the first step toward building a workforce capable of achieving their ambitious goals.

Back in his office, Jim reflected on the discussion. He knew that recruiting top talent was an ongoing process, but with the commitment and enthusiasm of his team, they were well on their way to building the foundation of a high-performing organization.

Fostering a Collaborative Culture

With the new recruitment strategies in place, Jim Cartwright turned his focus to fostering a collaborative culture at Cartwright Industries. He knew that to truly harness the potential of top talent, the company needed an environment where collaboration thrived. Today's meeting was dedicated to brainstorming ways to achieve this.

As the senior management team gathered in the boardroom, Jim sensed a mix of excitement and curiosity. He began the meeting with a sense of purpose.

"Good morning, everyone," Jim said, his voice calm but

resolute. "Now that we're on track to recruit top talent, our next goal is to foster a collaborative culture. Collaboration is the cornerstone of innovation and efficiency. It's essential for achieving our strategic vision."

He clicked the remote, revealing the slide titled **Fostering a Collaborative Culture: Strategies for Team Success**.

"Let's start by discussing what collaboration means to us," Jim continued. "How do we define it, and why is it important for our success?"

Diane Matthews, the CFO, spoke first. "Collaboration means working together across departments, sharing knowledge, and supporting each other to achieve common goals. It's important because it brings diverse perspectives and expertise to the table, leading to better decision-making and innovation."

Jim nodded. "Exactly. Collaboration isn't just about working together; it's about leveraging our collective strengths. So, how do we foster this kind of culture?"

Janet Ross, the HR Director, chimed in. "We need to start by creating opportunities for cross-departmental interactions. This can be through joint projects, team-building activities, and regular inter-departmental meetings."

Paul Bennett, the COO, added, "We should also promote a culture of open communication. This means encouraging employees to share their ideas and feedback without fear of judgment."

"Good points," Jim said, writing these down on the whiteboard. "What about the physical and virtual workspace? How can we design our work environment to promote collaboration?"

Richard Shaw, the head of sales, suggested, "We could

redesign our office layout to include more open spaces and collaboration zones. For remote teams, we need reliable communication tools and regular virtual meetings to ensure everyone stays connected."

Jim added this to the list. "And how do we ensure that collaboration becomes a core part of our culture, rather than just an occasional practice?"

Janet replied, "We need to lead by example. If the leadership team collaborates effectively, it sets the tone for the rest of the organization. Additionally, we should recognize and reward collaborative efforts to reinforce its importance."

"Excellent suggestions," Jim said, making more notes. "Now, let's talk about specific initiatives we can implement to promote collaboration."

He clicked to the next slide, which read: **Initiatives to Foster Collaboration**.

1. **Cross-Departmental Projects**
2. **Team-Building Activities**
3. **Open Communication Channels**
4. **Collaborative Workspaces**
5. **Leadership by Example**
6. **Recognition and Rewards**

"Let's flesh these out," Jim said. "For cross-departmental projects, what are some potential areas where we can bring teams together?"

Paul responded, "We could have teams from R&D, marketing, and sales work together on new product development. This would ensure that the product meets market demands and is effectively promoted."

"Great idea," Jim said. "And for team-building activities?"

Janet suggested, "We could organize regular off-site retreats, workshops, and social events to build stronger interpersonal relationships and trust among employees."

Jim nodded. "These activities will help break down silos and build a sense of camaraderie. What about open communication channels?"

Richard replied, "We should implement a company-wide intranet where employees can share ideas, ask questions, and collaborate on projects. Regular town hall meetings can also keep everyone informed and engaged."

"Excellent," Jim said. "For collaborative workspaces, we can redesign our office to include more open areas and meeting rooms equipped with the latest technology for virtual collaboration. And for leadership by example?"

Paul added, "We need to regularly demonstrate collaborative behavior in our meetings and decision-making processes. This means actively seeking input from different departments and working together to solve problems."

"Absolutely," Jim said. "Finally, for recognition and rewards?"

Diane suggested, "We could introduce a 'Collaborator of the Month' award to recognize employees who go above and beyond in working with others. Additionally, we can include collaboration as a key metric in performance reviews."

Jim made the final notes on the whiteboard. "These initiatives will help us build a truly collaborative culture. Remember, fostering collaboration is an ongoing effort. We need to be committed and consistent in promoting these values."

He looked around the room, seeing the enthusiasm in his team's faces. "Let's work together to implement these changes and create an environment where collaboration thrives."

As the meeting adjourned, Jim felt a renewed sense of purpose. With a clear strategy for fostering collaboration, he was confident that Cartwright Industries would become a more cohesive and innovative organization. This, he knew, was essential for achieving their strategic vision and building high-performing teams.

Back in his office, Jim reflected on the discussion. He knew that fostering a collaborative culture would require dedication and effort from everyone. But with the right initiatives and a committed team, he believed they could transform the company into a place where collaboration was not just encouraged but ingrained in their DNA.

Leadership Styles and Team Dynamics

Jim Cartwright understood that building high-performing teams required more than just recruiting top talent and fostering collaboration. It also involved understanding the different leadership styles and how they influenced team dynamics. Today, he was meeting with the senior management team to delve into this crucial aspect.

The boardroom was filled with anticipation as the team settled in. Jim stood at the front, ready to guide them through the discussion.

"Good morning, everyone," Jim began, his voice steady and confident. "Today, we're going to focus on leadership styles and how they affect team dynamics. Understanding this is key to building and maintaining high-performing teams."

He clicked the remote, and the slide titled **Leadership Styles and Team Dynamics: Guiding Teams to Success** appeared on the screen.

"Let's start by discussing the different leadership styles," Jim said. "What styles are we familiar with, and how do they impact team performance?"

Paul Bennett, the COO, spoke up. "We have the authoritarian style, where leaders make decisions unilaterally. This can lead to quick decision-making but might stifle creativity and lower morale if overused."

Jim nodded. "Exactly. Authoritarian leadership can be effective in crisis situations but isn't ideal for fostering innovation or collaboration. What other styles?"

Janet Ross, the HR Director, added, "There's the democratic style, where leaders involve team members in decision-making. This can boost morale and encourage input, but it might slow down the process."

"Good point," Jim said, making a note. "Democratic leadership fosters a sense of ownership and engagement but requires a balance to avoid decision paralysis. What about other styles?"

Diane Matthews, the CFO, chimed in. "There's also the transformational style, where leaders inspire and motivate their teams to exceed their own expectations. This can lead to high performance and innovation but requires a lot of energy and charisma from the leader."

Jim wrote this down. "Transformational leadership can indeed drive a team to great heights but needs sustained effort. Any others?"

Richard Shaw, the head of sales, mentioned, "Then there's the laissez-faire style, where leaders provide minimal direction and allow team members to make their own decisions. This can foster innovation and independence but might lead to a lack of direction."

Jim added it to the list. "Laissez-faire can be effective with highly skilled teams but needs to be monitored to ensure alignment with goals."

He clicked to the next slide, which read: **Impact of Leadership Styles on Team Dynamics**.

"Now, let's discuss how these styles impact team dynamics," Jim said. "How do different styles affect trust, communication, and performance?"

Paul replied, "Authoritarian leadership can create a clear structure but might lead to low trust and poor communication if team members feel their input isn't valued."

Janet added, "Democratic leadership can build trust and open communication, but it requires effective conflict resolution skills to manage differing opinions."

Diane mentioned, "Transformational leadership can inspire high performance and strong team loyalty, but it's important to ensure the leader remains approachable and open to feedback."

Richard said, "Laissez-faire leadership can promote independence and creativity, but it's crucial to have mechanisms in place to ensure team members remain aligned with the overall vision."

Jim nodded, summarizing their points on the whiteboard. "Understanding these dynamics is vital. We need to be flexible and adapt our leadership style to the needs of our team and the situation."

He turned to the next slide, which read: **Strategies for Effective Leadership and Team Dynamics**.

1. **Assess Team Needs**

2. **Adapt Leadership Style**
3. **Promote Open Communication**
4. **Encourage Feedback**
5. **Build Trust and Respect**
6. **Monitor and Adjust**

"Let's break these down," Jim said. "First, assessing team needs. How can we do this effectively?"

Janet suggested, "Regular one-on-one meetings and team surveys can help us understand individual and team needs better."

"Good idea," Jim said. "Next, adapting leadership style. How do we ensure we're using the right style at the right time?"

Paul responded, "We need to be aware of our natural leadership tendencies and be willing to adjust based on the situation and feedback from our team."

"Exactly," Jim said, making notes. "Promoting open communication. How do we foster an environment where team members feel comfortable sharing their thoughts?"

Diane replied, "We need to lead by example, showing that we value open communication and are approachable. Regular team meetings and open-door policies can also help."

Jim added this. "Encouraging feedback. How do we make sure feedback is constructive and welcomed?"

Richard suggested, "We should provide regular opportunities for feedback and act on it. This shows that we value it and are committed to improvement."

"Great," Jim said. "Building trust and respect. What are some ways we can achieve this?"

Janet replied, "Trust and respect are built over time through consistent actions. We need to be transparent, follow through on our commitments, and recognize team members' contributions."

Jim nodded. "Finally, monitoring and adjusting. How do we ensure we're continuously improving?"

Paul answered, "We should regularly review our leadership approaches and team dynamics, using performance metrics and feedback to make necessary adjustments."

Jim wrote the final point on the board. "These strategies will help us lead our teams effectively and create a positive dynamic. Remember, leadership is not a one-size-fits-all approach. We need to be adaptable and responsive to our team's needs."

He looked around the room, seeing the determination in his team's faces. "Let's commit to being flexible leaders who can adapt to any situation and foster a positive team dynamic. Together, we can build high-performing teams that drive our success."

As the meeting adjourned, Jim felt a renewed sense of confidence. With a clear understanding of leadership styles and their impact on team dynamics, he was certain that Cartwright Industries could cultivate a culture of high performance and collaboration. This, he knew, was essential for achieving their strategic vision and building a successful organization.

Back in his office, Jim reflected on the discussion. He knew that effective leadership required continuous learning and adaptation. But with the right strategies and a committed team, he believed they could navigate any challenges and lead Cartwright Industries to new heights.

Conflict Resolution Strategies

Jim Cartwright knew that even in the most collaborative environments, conflicts were inevitable. How these conflicts were resolved could either strengthen the team or create lasting rifts. Today's meeting with the senior management team was dedicated to discussing conflict resolution strategies to ensure that disagreements became opportunities for growth rather than obstacles.

The boardroom was filled with an undercurrent of anticipation as Jim entered. He sensed that this topic hit close to home for many, given the recent tensions between departments over resource allocation.

"Good morning, everyone," Jim began, his tone both serious and encouraging. "Today, we're going to tackle conflict resolution strategies. Conflict, if handled well, can lead to better understanding and innovation. If not, it can harm our productivity and morale."

He clicked the remote, and the slide titled **Conflict Resolution Strategies: Turning Challenges into Opportunities** appeared on the screen.

"Let's start by acknowledging that conflict is a natural part of any team dynamic," Jim said. "What kinds of conflicts have we encountered, and what was their impact?"

Paul Bennett, the COO, spoke first. "We've seen conflicts over resource allocation. Teams feel they're competing for limited resources, which creates tension and reduces cooperation."

Jim nodded. "That's a common issue. What else?"

Janet Ross, the HR Director, added, "There have also been conflicts related to differing work styles and communication preferences, particularly with our remote teams. This can lead to misunderstandings and frustration."

"Good points," Jim said, making notes. "And how have we been handling these conflicts so far?"

Diane Matthews, the CFO, chimed in, "Often, conflicts are addressed reactively. We step in when tensions boil over rather than addressing issues proactively."

Jim nodded again. "That's something we need to change. Effective conflict resolution should be proactive and constructive. Let's discuss some strategies to achieve this."

He clicked to the next slide, which read: **Key Conflict Resolution Strategies**.

1. **Open Communication**
2. **Active Listening**
3. **Identifying Root Causes**
4. **Collaborative Problem-Solving**
5. **Mediation and Facilitation**
6. **Follow-Up and Accountability**

"Let's break these down," Jim said. "First, open communication. How do we encourage team members to communicate openly about conflicts?"

Janet suggested, "We need to create a safe environment where team members feel comfortable voicing their concerns. This can be achieved through regular check-ins and team meetings where everyone is encouraged to speak up."

Jim nodded. "Good idea. Active listening is next. How can we ensure that we're truly listening to each other during conflicts?"

Paul responded, "We should practice active listening techniques, such as paraphrasing what the other person has said, asking clarifying questions, and showing empathy. This demonstrates that we value their perspective."

"Exactly," Jim said. "Identifying root causes. How do we get to the heart of the conflict rather than just addressing surface-level issues?"

Diane replied, "We need to dig deeper by asking open-ended questions and exploring underlying concerns and motivations. This helps us understand the real issues at play."

Jim added this to the list. "Collaborative problem-solving. How do we ensure that resolutions are mutually beneficial?"

Richard Shaw, the head of sales, suggested, "We should involve all parties in the resolution process, encouraging them to come up with solutions together. This fosters a sense of ownership and commitment to the resolution."

"Great," Jim said. "Mediation and facilitation. When should we bring in a neutral third party?"

Janet replied, "When conflicts are particularly complex or emotionally charged, a neutral mediator can help facilitate the discussion and ensure that all voices are heard. This can be someone from HR or an external mediator."

Jim made a note. "Finally, follow-up and accountability. How do we ensure that resolutions are implemented and sustained?"

Paul answered, "We should establish clear action items and timelines, and regularly check in to monitor progress. Holding everyone accountable ensures that conflicts don't resurface."

Jim clicked to the final slide, summarizing their strategies: encouraging open communication, practicing active listening, identifying root causes, promoting collaborative problem-solving, using mediation when necessary, and ensuring follow-up and accountability.

"These strategies will help us turn conflicts into opportunities for growth and improvement," Jim said. "Remember, the goal is not to avoid conflict but to handle it constructively."

He looked around the room, seeing the determination in his team's faces. "Let's commit to these strategies and create an environment where conflicts lead to positive change."

As the meeting adjourned, Jim felt a renewed sense of purpose. With clear strategies for conflict resolution, he was confident that Cartwright Industries could navigate disagreements effectively and build stronger, more cohesive teams.

Back in his office, Jim reflected on the discussion. He knew that effective conflict resolution required ongoing effort and commitment from everyone. But with the right strategies and a dedicated team, he believed they could transform conflicts into opportunities for learning and growth, ultimately strengthening the fabric of the organization.

Motivating and Retaining Employees

Jim Cartwright understood that building high-performing teams was not just about recruitment and conflict resolution—it also involved motivating and retaining talented employees. Today's meeting with the senior management team was dedicated to exploring strategies to keep their top talent engaged and committed for the long term.

The boardroom was filled with a sense of anticipation as Jim entered. He could see the eagerness in his team's eyes, knowing that this topic was crucial for the company's success.

"Good morning, everyone," Jim began, his voice filled with warmth and determination. "Today, we're going to discuss how we can motivate and retain our talented employees. Our success depends on their dedication and commitment."

He clicked the remote, and the slide titled **Motivating and Retaining Employees: Strategies for Long-Term Success** appeared on the screen.

"Let's start by acknowledging the importance of employee motivation," Jim said. "What motivates our employees, and how can we leverage those motivations to keep them engaged?"

Paul Bennett, the COO, spoke first. "Employees are motivated by more than just financial rewards. Recognition, opportunities for growth, and a sense of purpose are also important factors."

Jim nodded. "Absolutely. It's crucial that we understand what drives each individual and tailor our approach accordingly. What else?"

Janet Ross, the HR Director, added, "Employees also want to feel valued and appreciated. A positive work environment and supportive leadership can go a long way in boosting morale."

"Good point," Jim said, making notes. "And how do we ensure that our employees feel valued and appreciated?"

Diane Matthews, the CFO, chimed in, "Regular feedback and recognition are key. Employees want to know that their contributions are recognized and valued by their managers and peers."

Jim nodded again. "Recognition plays a significant role in employee motivation. What else?"

Richard Shaw, the head of sales, mentioned, "Opportunities for growth and development are also crucial. Employees want to feel like they're progressing in their careers and acquiring new skills."

"Absolutely," Jim said. "Providing opportunities for advancement and professional development not only motivates employees but also helps retain top talent. What else?"

Paul added, "A positive company culture and work-life balance are also important factors. Employees want to feel like they're part of something meaningful and that their well-being is valued."

Jim nodded, summarizing their points on the whiteboard. "Understanding these motivations is key to keeping our employees engaged and committed for the long term. Now, let's discuss some strategies to achieve this."

He clicked to the next slide, which read: **Key Strategies for Motivating and Retaining Employees**.

1. **Recognition and Appreciation**
2. **Opportunities for Growth and Development**
3. **Positive Company Culture**
4. **Work-Life Balance**
5. **Compensation and Benefits**
6. **Employee Well-Being Programs**

"Let's break these down," Jim said. "First, recognition and appreciation. How can we ensure that our employees feel valued for their contributions?"

Janet suggested, "We should implement regular recognition programs, such as 'Employee of the Month' awards or peer-to-peer recognition platforms. This shows employees that their hard work is noticed and appreciated."

Jim nodded. "Good idea. Opportunities for growth and

development. How can we provide avenues for employees to advance their careers?"

Diane replied, "We should offer training programs, mentorship opportunities, and career development plans tailored to each employee's goals. This shows that we're invested in their long-term success."

"Exactly," Jim said. "Positive company culture. How do we create an environment where employees feel connected and engaged?"

Richard suggested, "We should foster a culture of collaboration, trust, and transparency, where everyone feels like they're part of a team working toward a common goal. Regular team-building activities and social events can help strengthen these bonds."

Jim added this to the list. "Work-life balance. How do we ensure that our employees have time to recharge and pursue their interests outside of work?"

Paul answered, "We should encourage flexible work arrangements, such as telecommuting and flexible hours, to accommodate employees' personal needs. Additionally, we should promote a culture of taking breaks and vacations to prevent burnout."

"Good point," Jim said. "Compensation and benefits. How do we ensure that our employees feel fairly compensated for their work?"

Janet replied, "We should regularly review our compensation packages to ensure they're competitive in the market. Additionally, we should offer benefits that support employees' well-being, such as health insurance, retirement plans, and wellness programs."

Jim nodded. "Finally, employee well-being programs. How

do we prioritize our employees' physical and mental health?"

Diane suggested, "We should offer wellness initiatives, such as fitness programs, mental health resources, and stress management workshops. Additionally, we should provide access to counseling services and employee assistance programs."

Jim clicked to the final slide, summarizing their strategies: recognizing and appreciating employees, providing opportunities for growth and development, fostering a positive company culture, promoting work-life balance, offering competitive compensation and benefits, and prioritizing employee well-being.

"These strategies will help us create a workplace where employees feel valued, motivated, and fulfilled," Jim said. "Remember, our employees are our greatest asset. Let's invest in their success and well-being."

He looked around the room, seeing the determination in his team's faces. "Let's commit to implementing these strategies and creating an environment where our employees thrive."

As the meeting adjourned, Jim felt a renewed sense of purpose. With clear strategies for motivating and retaining employees, he was confident that Cartwright Industries could attract and retain top talent, ultimately driving the company's success.

Back in his office, Jim reflected on the discussion. He knew that keeping employees motivated and engaged required ongoing effort and commitment. But with the right strategies and a supportive culture, he believed they could create a workplace where employees felt valued, inspired, and excited to contribute to the company's mission.

Measuring Team Performance

Jim Cartwright understood that to build high-performing teams, it was crucial to have a clear understanding of their performance. Today's meeting with the senior management team was dedicated to discussing strategies for measuring and evaluating team performance to ensure they were on track to achieve their goals.

As Jim entered the boardroom, he could sense the anticipation in the air. The team was eager to delve into this important aspect of team dynamics.

"Good morning, everyone," Jim greeted, his voice firm yet welcoming. "Today, we're going to focus on measuring team performance. It's essential for us to have a clear understanding of how our teams are performing and where there may be areas for improvement."

He clicked the remote, and the slide titled **Measuring Team Performance: Strategies for Success** appeared on the screen.

"Let's start by discussing why it's important to measure team performance," Jim began. "What are the benefits of having a clear understanding of how our teams are performing?"

Paul Bennett, the COO, spoke up. "Measuring team performance allows us to identify strengths and weaknesses, allocate resources effectively, and make data-driven decisions to drive improvement."

Jim nodded. "Exactly. It also helps us track progress toward our goals and ensure that everyone is aligned with our strategic objectives. What else?"

Janet Ross, the HR Director, added, "Measuring team performance can also boost accountability and motivation.

When team members know that their performance is being evaluated, they're more likely to stay focused and committed to achieving results."

"Good points," Jim said, making notes. "And how do we ensure that our performance metrics are aligned with our strategic objectives?"

Diane Matthews, the CFO, chimed in, "We need to establish clear and measurable goals for each team that are directly tied to our overall strategic priorities. This ensures that everyone is working toward the same objectives."

Jim nodded again. "Absolutely. It's crucial that our performance metrics reflect what matters most to the success of the company. Now, let's discuss some strategies for measuring team performance effectively."

He clicked to the next slide, which read: **Key Strategies for Measuring Team Performance**.

1. **Establish Clear Goals and Objectives**
2. **Identify Key Performance Indicators (KPIs)**
3. **Regular Performance Reviews**
4. **Feedback and Coaching**
5. **Utilize Technology and Data Analytics**
6. **Continuous Improvement**

"Let's break these down," Jim said. "First, establishing clear goals and objectives. How do we ensure that our teams have a clear understanding of what they're working toward?"

Paul responded, "We should set SMART goals—specific, measurable, achievable, relevant, and time-bound—for each team, department, and individual. This provides a clear roadmap for success."

"Good idea," Jim said. "Next, identifying key performance indicators (KPIs). How do we determine which metrics are most important to track?"

Janet suggested, "We should identify KPIs that directly align with our strategic objectives and measure both quantitative and qualitative aspects of performance. This gives us a comprehensive view of how each team is contributing to our goals."

Jim nodded. "Regular performance reviews. How often should we evaluate team performance?"

Diane replied, "We should conduct regular performance reviews, such as quarterly or biannual assessments, to track progress, provide feedback, and identify areas for improvement."

"Exactly," Jim said. "Feedback and coaching. How do we ensure that our feedback is constructive and actionable?"

Richard Shaw, the head of sales, mentioned, "We should provide regular feedback to teams and individuals, focusing on both strengths and areas for improvement. Coaching sessions can help team members develop new skills and overcome challenges."

Jim added this to the list. "Utilize technology and data analytics. How can technology help us track and analyze team performance?"

Paul answered, "We should leverage project management software, data analytics tools, and other technology solutions to collect and analyze performance data in real-time. This allows us to make informed decisions and adjustments as needed."

"Great," Jim said. "Finally, continuous improvement. How do we ensure that we're constantly striving to improve team performance?"

Janet suggested, "We should foster a culture of continuous learning and development, encouraging teams to reflect on their performance, identify areas for growth, and implement strategies for improvement."

Jim clicked to the final slide, summarizing their strategies: setting clear goals and objectives, identifying key performance indicators, conducting regular performance reviews, providing feedback and coaching, utilizing technology and data analytics, and fostering a culture of continuous improvement.

"These strategies will help us measure team performance effectively and drive continuous improvement," Jim said. "Remember, our goal is not just to track performance but to use that data to enhance our teams' effectiveness and drive our strategic objectives."

He looked around the room, seeing the determination in his team's faces. "Let's commit to implementing these strategies and creating a culture of excellence and accountability."

As the meeting adjourned, Jim felt a renewed sense of purpose. With clear strategies for measuring team performance, he was confident that Cartwright Industries could achieve its goals and continue to grow and succeed.

Back in his office, Jim reflected on the discussion. He knew that measuring team performance was not just about collecting data—it was about using that data to drive improvement and achieve excellence. But with the right strategies and a committed team, he believed they could build a culture of continuous improvement that would propel the company to new heights.

4

Chapter 4: Financial Acumen for Executives

Understanding Financial Statements

J im Cartwright sat at the head of the table, his gaze focused and determined. Today's meeting with the senior management team was dedicated to imparting crucial knowledge: understanding financial statements. As the CFO began her presentation, Jim knew that mastering this topic was essential for every executive in the room.

"Good morning, everyone," Diane Matthews, the CFO, began, her voice commanding attention. "Today, we're going to dive into the fundamentals of understanding financial statements. As executives, it's crucial for us to be able to interpret these documents accurately to make informed decisions that drive the success of our company."

She clicked the remote, and the slide titled **Understanding Financial Statements: The Cornerstone of Financial Acumen** appeared on the screen.

"Let's start by discussing why financial statements are important," Diane continued. "What insights can we gain from these documents?"

Paul Bennett, the COO, spoke up. "Financial statements provide a snapshot of our company's financial health, including its profitability, liquidity, and solvency. They help us assess performance, identify trends, and make strategic decisions."

Diane nodded. "Exactly. Now, let's delve into the components of financial statements. The three main statements are the balance sheet, income statement, and cash flow statement."

She clicked to the next slide, which displayed the definitions of each statement.

"The balance sheet," Diane explained, "provides a snapshot of the company's financial position at a specific point in time, including its assets, liabilities, and equity."

Janet Ross, the HR Director, raised her hand. "What are assets, liabilities, and equity, exactly?"

Diane smiled. "Great question. Assets are what the company owns or controls, such as cash, inventory, and property. Liabilities are what the company owes to creditors, such as loans and accounts payable. Equity represents the company's ownership interests, including shareholders' equity and retained earnings."

She continued to explain each component in detail, using real-world examples and scenarios to illustrate her points.

"Next," Diane said, "we have the income statement, also known as the profit and loss statement. This document shows the company's revenues and expenses over a specific period, typically a quarter or a year."

Richard Shaw, the head of sales, nodded. "So, the income statement tells us whether we're making a profit or a loss?"

"Exactly," Diane confirmed. "It shows us our net income, which is the difference between our revenues and expenses. A positive net income indicates profit, while a negative net income indicates loss."

Finally, Diane moved on to the cash flow statement. "This statement shows how cash flows in and out of the company over a specific period. It provides insights into the company's operating, investing, and financing activities."

As she explained each section of the cash flow statement, Jim could see the pieces falling into place for his team. Understanding financial statements was crucial for making strategic decisions that would drive the company's success.

After Diane's presentation concluded, Jim thanked her for her insightful overview. "Understanding financial statements is essential for every executive in this room. It's the foundation of financial acumen, and mastering it will empower us to make informed decisions that drive our company forward."

As the meeting adjourned, Jim could sense a newfound confidence in his team. They now had the tools and knowledge to navigate the complexities of financial statements and use them to steer Cartwright Industries toward greater success.

Budgeting and Forecasting

As the discussion on financial acumen continued, Jim Cartwright shifted the focus to another critical aspect: budgeting and forecasting. He knew that understanding these concepts was essential for effective financial management and decision-making at Cartwright Industries.

"Good morning, everyone," Jim began, his tone firm yet inviting. "Today, we're going to delve into budgeting and forecasting—two key practices that play a crucial role in our financial planning and strategic decision-making processes."

He clicked the remote, and the slide titled **Budgeting and Forecasting: Driving Financial Stability and Growth** appeared on the screen.

"Let's start by discussing why budgeting and forecasting are important," Jim continued. "What are the benefits of having a clear budget and forecast?"

Paul Bennett, the COO, spoke up. "Budgeting and forecasting help us set financial goals, allocate resources effectively, and monitor our performance against targets. They provide a roadmap for our financial activities and help ensure that we're on track to achieve our strategic objectives."

Jim nodded. "Exactly. Now, let's delve into each of these practices in more detail."

He clicked to the next slide, which displayed **Budgeting**.

"The budget," Jim explained, "is a financial plan that outlines our expected revenues and expenses over a specific period, typically a year. It serves as a guideline for our financial activities and helps us allocate resources in line with our strategic priorities."

Janet Ross, the HR Director, raised her hand. "How do we create a budget?"

Jim smiled. "Great question. Creating a budget involves forecasting our revenues and expenses based on historical data, market trends, and strategic plans. We then allocate resources to different departments and projects based on these forecasts."

He continued to explain the budgeting process in detail, emphasizing the importance of collaboration and communication across departments.

"Next," Jim said, clicking to the next slide, "we have **Forecasting**."

"The forecast," he explained, "is an estimate of future financial performance based on past data and current trends. It helps us anticipate potential challenges and opportunities and adjust our plans accordingly."

Richard Shaw, the head of sales, nodded. "So, forecasting helps us predict how our business will perform in the future?"

"Exactly," Jim confirmed. "It allows us to identify potential risks and opportunities early on and take proactive measures to mitigate risks and capitalize on opportunities."

He continued to explain various forecasting techniques, such as trend analysis, regression analysis, and scenario planning, using real-world examples to illustrate their application.

"As executives," Jim concluded, "it's essential for us to understand the principles of budgeting and forecasting. These practices provide us with valuable insights into our financial health and help us make informed decisions that drive our company's stability and growth."

After Jim's presentation concluded, the room buzzed with discussion as the team members exchanged ideas and insights. They now had a clearer understanding of budgeting and forecasting and were ready to apply this knowledge to their strategic planning efforts.

As the meeting adjourned, Jim felt a sense of satisfaction. With a solid grasp of budgeting and forecasting, he knew that his team was better equipped to navigate the financial complexities of Cartwright Industries and drive its success forward.

Managing Financial Risks

With the foundation of budgeting and forecasting laid, Jim Cartwright turned the attention of the senior management team to another critical aspect of financial acumen: managing financial risks. He knew that understanding and mitigating risks was essential for safeguarding the financial stability and growth of Cartwright Industries.

"Good morning, everyone," Jim began, his tone serious yet focused. "Today, we're going to discuss managing financial risks—a crucial aspect of financial acumen that requires our attention and expertise."

He clicked the remote, and the slide titled **Managing Financial Risks: Safeguarding Our Future** appeared on the screen.

"Let's start by discussing why managing financial risks is important," Jim continued. "What are the potential risks that our company faces, and how do they impact our financial health?"

Paul Bennett, the COO, spoke up. "Financial risks can come in many forms, such as market volatility, credit risk, liquidity risk, and operational risk. These risks can negatively impact our profitability, cash flow, and overall financial stability."

Jim nodded. "Exactly. Now, let's delve into each of these risks and discuss strategies for managing them effectively."

He clicked to the next slide, which displayed **Types of Financial Risks**.

"The first type of risk," Jim explained, "is **Market Risk**. This refers to the risk of financial losses due to changes in market conditions, such as fluctuations in interest rates, exchange rates, or commodity prices."

Janet Ross, the HR Director, raised her hand. "How do we mitigate market risk?"

Jim smiled. "Great question. Mitigating market risk involves diversifying our investments, hedging against adverse movements in market prices, and staying informed about market trends and developments."

He continued to explain various strategies for managing market risk, such as using derivatives, forward contracts, and options to hedge against adverse market movements.

"Next," Jim said, clicking to the next slide, "we have **Credit Risk**."

"Credit risk," he explained, "refers to the risk of financial loss due to the failure of a borrower to repay a loan or meet their financial obligations. This can occur when customers default on payments or when counterparties fail to fulfill their contractual obligations."

Richard Shaw, the head of sales, nodded. "How do we mitigate credit risk?"

"Mitigating credit risk," Jim replied, "involves conducting thorough credit assessments of customers and counterparties, setting credit limits, and implementing effective credit monitoring and collection processes."

He continued to explain various strategies for managing credit risk, such as diversifying the customer base, obtaining credit insurance, and using collateral to secure loans.

"As executives," Jim concluded, "it's essential for us to identify and mitigate financial risks effectively. By doing so, we can safeguard the financial stability and growth of Cartwright Industries and protect our stakeholders' interests."

After Jim's presentation concluded, the room buzzed with discussion as the team members exchanged ideas and insights.

They now had a clearer understanding of managing financial risks and were ready to apply this knowledge to their decision-making processes.

As the meeting adjourned, Jim felt a sense of reassurance. With a solid grasp of managing financial risks, he knew that his team was better equipped to navigate the financial challenges ahead and ensure the continued success of Cartwright Industries.

Investment and Capital Allocation

With the discussion on managing financial risks concluded, Jim Cartwright shifted the focus of the senior management team to another critical aspect of financial acumen: investment and capital allocation. He knew that making strategic investment decisions and effectively allocating capital were essential for driving the growth and success of Cartwright Industries.

"Good morning, everyone," Jim began, his voice carrying authority. "Today, we're going to explore investment and capital allocation—two key practices that play a crucial role in our company's financial strategy and long-term success."

He clicked the remote, and the slide titled **Investment and Capital Allocation: Fueling Growth and Innovation** appeared on the screen.

"Let's start by discussing why investment and capital allocation are important," Jim continued. "What are the potential benefits of making strategic investments and allocating capital effectively?"

Paul Bennett, the COO, spoke up. "Strategic investments and capital allocation can drive growth, increase profitability, and enhance shareholder value. By investing in projects and initiatives that generate high returns, we can maximize the value of our capital and position our company for long-term success."

Jim nodded. "Exactly. Now, let's delve into each of these practices in more detail."

He clicked to the next slide, which displayed **Strategic Investments**.

"The first practice," Jim explained, "is making strategic investments. This involves allocating capital to projects, initiatives, or assets that have the potential to generate high returns and create long-term value for the company."

Janet Ross, the HR Director, raised her hand. "How do we identify strategic investment opportunities?"

Jim smiled. "Great question. Identifying strategic investment opportunities involves conducting thorough analysis and due diligence to assess the potential risks and rewards of each investment. We need to consider factors such as market trends, competitive dynamics, and the company's strategic objectives."

He continued to explain various criteria for evaluating strategic investment opportunities, such as return on investment (ROI), payback period, and risk-adjusted return.

"Next," Jim said, clicking to the next slide, "we have **Capital Allocation**."

"Capital allocation," he explained, "refers to the process of determining how to deploy the company's financial resources across different projects, initiatives, or business units. It involves prioritizing investment opportunities based on their potential to create value and achieve strategic objectives."

Richard Shaw, the head of sales, nodded. "How do we

prioritize capital allocation decisions?"

"Prioritizing capital allocation decisions," Jim replied, "involves assessing each opportunity based on its alignment with the company's strategic goals, its potential for generating returns, and its risk profile. We need to allocate capital to projects that offer the highest return on investment and contribute most effectively to our long-term growth and profitability."

He continued to explain various strategies for capital allocation, such as portfolio optimization, resource allocation frameworks, and capital budgeting techniques.

"As executives," Jim concluded, "it's essential for us to make strategic investments and allocate capital effectively. By doing so, we can drive growth, enhance profitability, and create long-term value for Cartwright Industries and its stakeholders."

After Jim's presentation concluded, the room buzzed with discussion as the team members exchanged ideas and insights. They now had a clearer understanding of investment and capital allocation and were ready to apply this knowledge to their strategic decision-making processes.

As the meeting adjourned, Jim felt a sense of confidence. With a solid grasp of investment and capital allocation principles, he knew that his team was better equipped to make strategic decisions that would drive the growth and success of Cartwright Industries in the years to come.

Cost Reduction Strategies

With the discussion on investment and capital allocation concluded, Jim Cartwright turned the attention of the senior management team to another critical aspect of financial acumen: cost reduction strategies. He knew that effectively managing costs was essential for maintaining profitability and driving efficiency at Cartwright Industries.

"Good morning, everyone," Jim began, his voice steady and authoritative. "Today, we're going to explore cost reduction strategies—a key practice that plays a crucial role in our company's financial health and competitiveness."

He clicked the remote, and the slide titled **Cost Reduction Strategies: Maximizing Efficiency and Profitability** appeared on the screen.

"Let's start by discussing why cost reduction strategies are important," Jim continued. "What are the potential benefits of reducing costs and improving efficiency?"

Paul Bennett, the COO, spoke up. "Cost reduction strategies can help us improve profitability, increase cash flow, and enhance our competitive position in the market. By reducing unnecessary expenses and improving operational efficiency, we can maximize the value we deliver to our customers and shareholders."

Jim nodded. "Exactly. Now, let's delve into some effective cost reduction strategies."

He clicked to the next slide, which displayed **Key Cost Reduction Strategies**.

"The first strategy," Jim explained, "is **Identifying Cost Drivers**. This involves analyzing our cost structure to identify the key drivers of our expenses and prioritize areas for cost reduction."

Janet Ross, the HR Director, raised her hand. "How do we identify cost drivers?"

Jim smiled. "Great question. Identifying cost drivers involves conducting a comprehensive analysis of our operations, processes, and expenditures to understand where the majority of our costs are incurred. We need to focus on areas where we can achieve the greatest cost savings with the least impact on our business operations."

He continued to explain various methods for identifying cost drivers, such as activity-based costing, value stream mapping, and cost-volume-profit analysis.

"Next," Jim said, clicking to the next slide, "we have **Stream-lining Processes**."

"Streamlining processes," he explained, "involves optimizing our workflows, eliminating unnecessary steps, and automating repetitive tasks to improve efficiency and reduce costs."

Richard Shaw, the head of sales, nodded. "How do we streamline processes effectively?"

"Streamlining processes effectively," Jim replied, "requires collaboration across departments and a focus on continuous improvement. We need to identify bottlenecks and inefficiencies in our workflows and implement solutions to streamline operations and reduce costs."

He continued to explain various strategies for streamlining processes, such as implementing lean principles, investing in technology and automation, and standardizing workflows.

"As executives," Jim concluded, "it's essential for us to prioritize cost reduction and efficiency improvement initiatives. By identifying cost drivers, streamlining processes, and implementing other cost reduction strategies, we can enhance our competitiveness and drive long-term success for Cartwright Industries."

After Jim's presentation concluded, the room buzzed with discussion as the team members exchanged ideas and insights. They now had a clearer understanding of cost reduction strategies and were ready to apply this knowledge to their operations to drive efficiency and profitability.

As the meeting adjourned, Jim felt a sense of determination. With a solid grasp of cost reduction principles, he knew that his team was better equipped to identify opportunities for improvement and drive positive change at Cartwright Industries.

Financial Decision-Making

With the discussion on cost reduction strategies concluded, Jim Cartwright turned the focus of the senior management team to another critical aspect of financial acumen: financial decision-making. He knew that making sound financial decisions was essential for driving the success and sustainability of Cartwright Industries.

"Good morning, everyone," Jim began, his tone commanding attention. "Today, we're going to explore financial decision-making—a key practice that shapes the financial health and future trajectory of our company."

He clicked the remote, and the slide titled **Financial Decision-Making: Navigating Complexity with Confidence** appeared on the screen.

"Let's start by discussing why financial decision-making is important," Jim continued. "What are the potential impacts of our financial decisions on the company's performance and success?"

Paul Bennett, the COO, spoke up. "Financial decisions can have significant implications for our company's profitability, cash flow, and overall financial health. They can impact our ability to invest in growth opportunities, manage risks effectively, and create value for our shareholders."

Jim nodded. "Exactly. Now, let's delve into some key principles of financial decision-making."

He clicked to the next slide, which displayed **Principles of Financial Decision-Making**.

"The first principle," Jim explained, "is **Data-Driven Decision-Making**. This involves gathering and analyzing relevant financial data to inform our decision-making process and ensure that our decisions are based on accurate information and insights."

Janet Ross, the HR Director, raised her hand. "How do we ensure that our financial decisions are data-driven?"

Jim smiled. "Great question. Ensuring that our financial decisions are data-driven involves collecting and analyzing financial data from various sources, such as financial statements, market research, and economic indicators. We need to use this data to assess the potential risks and rewards of each decision and make informed choices that align with our strategic objectives."

He continued to explain various methods for gathering and analyzing financial data, such as financial modeling, scenario analysis, and sensitivity analysis.

"Next," Jim said, clicking to the next slide, "we have **Risk Management**."

"Risk management," he explained, "involves identifying, assessing, and mitigating financial risks associated with our decisions to protect the company's financial interests and ensure its long-term sustainability."

Richard Shaw, the head of sales, nodded. "How do we manage financial risks effectively?"

"Managing financial risks effectively," Jim replied, "requires a proactive approach to identifying potential risks and implementing strategies to mitigate them. We need to assess the impact of our decisions on factors such as market volatility, credit risk, and liquidity risk, and take steps to minimize their adverse effects on the company."

He continued to explain various strategies for managing financial risks, such as diversification, hedging, and insurance.

"As executives," Jim concluded, "it's essential for us to approach financial decision-making with rigor and discipline. By adhering to principles such as data-driven decision-making and risk management, we can make informed choices that drive the success and sustainability of Cartwright Industries."

After Jim's presentation concluded, the room buzzed with discussion as the team members exchanged ideas and insights. They now had a clearer understanding of financial decision-making and were ready to apply this knowledge to their strategic planning efforts.

As the meeting adjourned, Jim felt a sense of confidence. With a solid grasp of financial decision-making principles, he knew that his team was better equipped to navigate the complexities of financial management and drive the success of Cartwright Industries into the future.

5

Chapter 5: Effective Decision-Making

Decision-Making Frameworks

J im Cartwright, seated at the head of the conference table, addressed the senior management team with a sense of purpose. Today's focus was on effective decision-making, a cornerstone of leadership within Cartwright Industries.

"Good morning, everyone," Jim greeted, his voice resonating with authority. "Today, we embark on a journey to explore effective decision-making—an essential skill for navigating the complexities of our industry and driving the success of Cartwright Industries."

He clicked the remote, and the slide titled **Effective Decision-Making: Guiding Our Path Forward** illuminated the screen.

"Let's begin by understanding why effective decision-making is paramount," Jim continued. "What are the repercussions of our decisions on the company's trajectory?"

Paul Bennett, the COO, spoke up. "Our decisions shape

the direction of the company, influencing everything from our competitive positioning to our financial performance. Effective decision-making ensures that we capitalize on opportunities and mitigate risks."

Jim nodded in agreement. "Precisely. Now, let's delve into decision-making frameworks."

He clicked to the next slide, which displayed **Decision-Making Frameworks**.

"The first framework," Jim explained, "is **Rational Decision-Making**. This approach involves a systematic process of defining objectives, gathering relevant information, evaluating alternatives, and choosing the best course of action based on logic and reason."

Janet Ross, the HR Director, raised a question. "How do we ensure that our decisions follow a rational approach?"

Jim acknowledged her inquiry. "Ensuring rational decision-making involves setting clear objectives, conducting thorough analysis, and considering both quantitative and qualitative factors. We must weigh the potential risks and rewards of each option before making a decision."

He continued to elaborate on the rational decision-making process, emphasizing the importance of data-driven insights and critical thinking.

"Next," Jim said, clicking to the next slide, "we have **Intuitive Decision-Making**."

"Intuitive decision-making," he explained, "relies on gut feelings, instincts, and past experiences to guide decision-making. While it may seem less systematic than the rational approach, intuition can be a valuable tool, especially in situations where time is limited or information is incomplete."

Richard Shaw, the head of sales, nodded in agreement.

"How do we balance rationality and intuition in our decision-making?"

"Balancing rationality and intuition," Jim replied, "requires self-awareness and mindfulness. We must be open to intuitive insights while also subjecting our decisions to rational scrutiny to ensure they align with our objectives and values."

He continued to discuss the strengths and limitations of intuitive decision-making, highlighting scenarios where it can complement rational analysis.

"As executives," Jim concluded, "we must leverage decision-making frameworks to guide our choices and drive the success of Cartwright Industries. By combining rational analysis with intuitive insights, we can make informed decisions that propel our company forward."

After Jim's presentation concluded, the room buzzed with discussion as the team members exchanged ideas and insights. They now had a clearer understanding of decision-making frameworks and were ready to apply this knowledge to their leadership roles within the company.

As the meeting adjourned, Jim felt a sense of optimism. With a solid grasp of effective decision-making principles, he knew that his team was better equipped to tackle the challenges and opportunities that lay ahead for Cartwright Industries.

Data-Driven Decisions

As the discussion on decision-making frameworks concluded, Jim Cartwright shifted the focus of the senior management team to another critical aspect: data-driven decisions. He knew that leveraging data to inform decision-making was essential for driving the success and innovation of Cartwright

Industries.

"Good morning, everyone," Jim began, his tone filled with determination. "Today, we're going to explore data-driven decisions—an essential practice that empowers us to make informed choices based on evidence and insights."

He clicked the remote, and the slide titled **Data-Driven Decisions: Empowering Insightful Choices** appeared on the screen.

"Let's start by understanding why data-driven decisions are crucial," Jim continued. "What are the advantages of leveraging data to inform our choices?"

Paul Bennett, the COO, spoke up. "Data-driven decisions allow us to uncover trends, patterns, and opportunities that may not be apparent through intuition alone. By analyzing data, we can make more accurate predictions, identify areas for improvement, and drive innovation."

Jim nodded in agreement. "Precisely. Now, let's delve into the principles of data-driven decisions."

He clicked to the next slide, which displayed **Principles of Data-Driven Decisions**.

"The first principle," Jim explained, "is **Collecting Relevant Data**. This involves gathering accurate and reliable data from various sources, such as internal systems, market research, and customer feedback, to provide a comprehensive view of the decision-making context."

Janet Ross, the HR Director, raised a question. "How do we ensure that we collect relevant data?"

Jim acknowledged her inquiry. "Ensuring that we collect relevant data involves defining clear objectives for our decision-making process and identifying the key metrics and indicators that will help us measure progress and evaluate outcomes."

He continued to elaborate on the importance of data collection methods, such as surveys, interviews, and analytics tools, to gather insights effectively.

"Next," Jim said, clicking to the next slide, "we have **Analyzing Data**."

"Analyzing data," he explained, "involves transforming raw data into actionable insights through statistical analysis, data visualization, and interpretation. By examining patterns, correlations, and trends in the data, we can uncover valuable insights that inform our decision-making process."

Richard Shaw, the head of sales, nodded in agreement. "How do we ensure that our data analysis is robust?"

"Ensuring robust data analysis," Jim replied, "requires a combination of technical expertise, critical thinking, and domain knowledge. We must use appropriate analytical techniques and tools to interpret the data accurately and avoid common pitfalls such as bias and misinterpretation."

He continued to discuss the importance of data analysis techniques, such as regression analysis, correlation analysis, and predictive modeling, to derive meaningful insights from the data.

"As executives," Jim concluded, "it's essential for us to embrace data-driven decision-making as a core practice. By collecting relevant data and analyzing it effectively, we can make informed choices that drive the success and innovation of Cartwright Industries."

After Jim's presentation concluded, the room buzzed with discussion as the team members exchanged ideas and insights. They now had a clearer understanding of data-driven decision-making and were ready to apply this knowledge to their leadership roles within the company.

As the meeting adjourned, Jim felt a sense of confidence. With a solid grasp of data-driven decision-making principles, he knew that his team was better equipped to leverage data as a strategic asset and drive the success of Cartwright Industries into the future.

Balancing Risk and Reward

With the discussion on data-driven decisions concluded, Jim Cartwright shifted the focus of the senior management team to another critical aspect: balancing risk and reward. He knew that finding the right balance between risk-taking and reward-seeking was essential for driving innovation and growth at Cartwright Industries.

"Good morning, everyone," Jim began, his voice resonating with purpose. "Today, we're going to explore the delicate art of balancing risk and reward—an essential practice that defines our approach to decision-making and drives our company's success."

He clicked the remote, and the slide titled **Balancing Risk and Reward: Navigating Uncertainty with Confidence** appeared on the screen.

"Let's start by understanding why balancing risk and reward is crucial," Jim continued. "What are the implications of our risk-taking decisions on the company's growth and profitability?"

Paul Bennett, the COO, spoke up. "Balancing risk and reward allows us to pursue growth opportunities while mitigating potential risks that could jeopardize our financial stability. It ensures that we make informed decisions that align with our strategic objectives and deliver value to our stakeholders."

Jim nodded in agreement. "Exactly. Now, let's delve into the principles of balancing risk and reward."

He clicked to the next slide, which displayed **Principles of Balancing Risk and Reward**.

"The first principle," Jim explained, "is **Risk Assessment**. This involves evaluating the potential risks associated with a decision, such as market volatility, competitive threats, and regulatory changes, to determine the likelihood and impact of adverse outcomes."

Janet Ross, the HR Director, raised a question. "How do we assess risk effectively?"

Jim acknowledged her inquiry. "Assessing risk effectively involves identifying potential risks, analyzing their potential impact on our objectives, and prioritizing them based on their likelihood and severity. We must also consider our risk tolerance and appetite for uncertainty when making decisions."

He continued to elaborate on the importance of risk assessment techniques, such as risk matrices, scenario analysis, and sensitivity analysis, to evaluate and mitigate risks effectively.

"Next," Jim said, clicking to the next slide, "we have **Reward Evaluation**."

"Reward evaluation," he explained, "involves assessing the potential rewards and benefits associated with a decision, such as revenue growth, cost savings, and competitive advantage, to determine the potential upside of pursuing a particular course of action."

Richard Shaw, the head of sales, nodded in agreement. "How do we evaluate rewards effectively?"

"Evaluating rewards effectively," Jim replied, "requires a

thorough analysis of the potential benefits and returns associated with a decision, taking into account both quantitative and qualitative factors. We must also consider the long-term implications of our decisions on the company's strategic objectives and competitive positioning."

He continued to discuss the importance of reward evaluation techniques, such as cost-benefit analysis, return on investment (ROI), and net present value (NPV), to assess the potential upside of pursuing different options.

"As executives," Jim concluded, "it's essential for us to strike the right balance between risk and reward in our decision-making process. By assessing risks effectively and evaluating rewards carefully, we can make informed choices that drive innovation and growth at Cartwright Industries."

After Jim's presentation concluded, the room buzzed with discussion as the team members exchanged ideas and insights. They now had a clearer understanding of balancing risk and reward and were ready to apply this knowledge to their leadership roles within the company.

As the meeting adjourned, Jim felt a sense of optimism. With a solid grasp of risk and reward principles, he knew that his team was better equipped to navigate the uncertainties of decision-making and drive the success of Cartwright Industries into the future.

Involving Stakeholders

As the discussion on balancing risk and reward concluded, Jim Cartwright shifted the focus of the senior management team to another critical aspect: involving stakeholders in the decision-making process. He knew that engaging stakeholders was essential for building consensus, gaining valuable insights, and fostering a sense of ownership in decision outcomes at Cartwright Industries.

"Good morning, everyone," Jim began, his tone warm yet authoritative. "Today, we're going to explore the importance of involving stakeholders in our decision-making process—an essential practice that drives collaboration, transparency, and alignment within our organization."

He clicked the remote, and the slide titled **Involving Stakeholders: Harnessing Collective Wisdom** appeared on the screen.

"Let's start by understanding why involving stakeholders is crucial," Jim continued. "What are the benefits of engaging stakeholders in our decision-making process?"

Paul Bennett, the COO, spoke up. "Involving stakeholders allows us to tap into their diverse perspectives, expertise, and insights, enriching our decision-making process and increasing the likelihood of successful implementation. It also builds trust, buy-in, and commitment among our stakeholders, fostering a culture of collaboration and shared responsibility."

Jim nodded in agreement. "Exactly. Now, let's delve into the principles of involving stakeholders."

He clicked to the next slide, which displayed **Principles of Involving Stakeholders**.

"The first principle," Jim explained, "is **Identifying Stakeholders**. This involves identifying all individuals and groups who may be affected by or have a vested interest in the decision, such as employees, customers, suppliers, investors, and regulators."

Janet Ross, the HR Director, raised a question. "How do we identify stakeholders effectively?"

Jim acknowledged her inquiry. "Identifying stakeholders effectively involves conducting stakeholder analysis to map out their interests, influence, and potential impact on the decision. We must also consider their level of involvement and engagement throughout the decision-making process."

He continued to elaborate on the importance of stakeholder identification techniques, such as stakeholder mapping, surveys, and interviews, to ensure that all relevant perspectives are considered.

"Next," Jim said, clicking to the next slide, "we have **Engaging Stakeholders**."

"Engaging stakeholders," he explained, "involves involving them in the decision-making process through open communication, collaboration, and participation. We must provide stakeholders with opportunities to share their views, provide feedback, and contribute to the decision-making process."

Richard Shaw, the head of sales, nodded in agreement. "How do we engage stakeholders effectively?"

"Engaging stakeholders effectively," Jim replied, "requires clear and transparent communication, active listening, and meaningful involvement in decision-making forums such as meetings, workshops, and focus groups. We must also provide stakeholders with timely and relevant information to enable informed participation."

He continued to discuss the importance of stakeholder engagement techniques, such as town hall meetings, advisory boards, and online forums, to foster collaboration and build consensus.

"As executives," Jim concluded, "it's essential for us to involve stakeholders in our decision-making process. By identifying stakeholders, engaging them effectively, and considering their perspectives, we can make decisions that are informed, inclusive, and ultimately more successful."

After Jim's presentation concluded, the room buzzed with discussion as the team members exchanged ideas and insights. They now had a clearer understanding of involving stakeholders and were ready to apply this knowledge to their leadership roles within the company.

As the meeting adjourned, Jim felt a sense of satisfaction. With a solid grasp of stakeholder involvement principles, he knew that his team was better equipped to harness the collective wisdom of Cartwright Industries and drive the success of the organization into the future.

Evaluating Outcomes

With the discussion on involving stakeholders concluded, Jim Cartwright shifted the focus of the senior management team to another critical aspect: evaluating outcomes. He knew that assessing the results of decisions was essential for learning, improvement, and accountability at Cartwright Industries.

"Good morning, everyone," Jim began, his voice filled with purpose. "Today, we're going to explore the importance of evaluating outcomes—an essential practice that allows us to learn from our decisions, adapt to changing circumstances, and drive continuous improvement."

He clicked the remote, and the slide titled **Evaluating Outcomes: Learning from Experience** appeared on the screen.

"Let's start by understanding why evaluating outcomes is crucial," Jim continued. "What are the benefits of assessing the results of our decisions?"

Paul Bennett, the COO, spoke up. "Evaluating outcomes allows us to assess the effectiveness of our decisions, identify areas for improvement, and learn from both our successes and failures. It enables us to refine our strategies, optimize our processes, and drive better results in the future."

Jim nodded in agreement. "Exactly. Now, let's delve into the principles of evaluating outcomes."

He clicked to the next slide, which displayed **Principles of Evaluating Outcomes**.

"The first principle," Jim explained, "is **Defining Success Metrics**. This involves establishing clear and measurable criteria for evaluating the outcomes of our decisions, such as key performance indicators (KPIs), targets, and benchmarks."

Janet Ross, the HR Director, raised a question. "How do we define success metrics effectively?"

Jim acknowledged her inquiry. "Defining success metrics effectively involves aligning them with our strategic objectives and ensuring that they are specific, relevant, and achievable. We must also consider the timeframe for evaluation and establish a baseline for comparison."

He continued to elaborate on the importance of success metrics, emphasizing the need for alignment with organizational goals and objectives.

"Next," Jim said, clicking to the next slide, "we have **Analyzing Results**."

"Analyzing results," he explained, "involves examining the data and evidence collected during the evaluation process to assess the outcomes of our decisions objectively. We must analyze both quantitative and qualitative data to gain a comprehensive understanding of the impact of our decisions."

Richard Shaw, the head of sales, nodded in agreement. "How

do we analyze results effectively?"

"Analyzing results effectively," Jim replied, "requires a rigorous and systematic approach to data analysis, using appropriate techniques and tools to derive meaningful insights. We must also consider the context and circumstances surrounding the decision to ensure that our analysis is accurate and relevant."

He continued to discuss the importance of data analysis techniques, such as trend analysis, root cause analysis, and variance analysis, to assess the outcomes of decisions accurately.

"As executives," Jim concluded, "it's essential for us to evaluate outcomes systematically and objectively. By defining success metrics, analyzing results, and learning from our experiences, we can drive continuous improvement and enhance the effectiveness of our decision-making process."

After Jim's presentation concluded, the room buzzed with discussion as the team members exchanged ideas and insights. They now had a clearer understanding of evaluating outcomes and were ready to apply this knowledge to their leadership roles within the company.

As the meeting adjourned, Jim felt a sense of satisfaction. With a solid grasp of outcome evaluation principles, he knew that his team was better equipped to learn from their experiences and drive the success of Cartwright Industries into the future.

Learning from Mistakes

With the discussion on evaluating outcomes concluded, Jim Cartwright shifted the focus of the senior management team to another critical aspect: learning from mistakes. He knew that acknowledging and addressing failures was essential for fostering a culture of innovation, resilience, and continuous improvement at Cartwright Industries.

"Good morning, everyone," Jim began, his tone compassionate yet determined. "Today, we're going to explore the importance of learning from mistakes—an essential practice that allows us to grow, adapt, and thrive in the face of adversity."

He clicked the remote, and the slide titled **Learning from Mistakes: Embracing Failure as an Opportunity** appeared on the screen.

"Let's start by understanding why learning from mistakes is crucial," Jim continued. "What are the benefits of acknowledging and addressing our failures?"

Paul Bennett, the COO, spoke up. "Learning from mistakes allows us to identify areas for improvement, refine our strategies, and build resilience in the face of challenges. It fosters a culture of innovation and continuous improvement, where failures are viewed as opportunities for growth rather than setbacks."

Jim nodded in agreement. "Precisely. Now, let's delve into the principles of learning from mistakes."

He clicked to the next slide, which displayed **Principles of Learning from Mistakes**.

"The first principle," Jim explained, "is **Creating a Safe Environment**. This involves fostering a culture where

94

employees feel safe to take risks, make mistakes, and learn from failure without fear of retribution or blame."

Janet Ross, the HR Director, raised a question. "How do we create a safe environment for learning from mistakes?"

Jim acknowledged her inquiry. "Creating a safe environment involves promoting psychological safety, encouraging open communication, and leading by example. We must demonstrate vulnerability and humility as leaders, acknowledging our own mistakes and embracing feedback as an opportunity for growth."

He continued to elaborate on the importance of psychological safety, emphasizing the need for trust, respect, and empathy in the workplace.

"Next," Jim said, clicking to the next slide, "we have **Analyzing Root Causes**."

"Analyzing root causes," he explained, "involves conducting a thorough investigation to understand the underlying factors that contributed to the failure. We must identify the root causes of our mistakes to address systemic issues and prevent similar failures from occurring in the future."

Richard Shaw, the head of sales, nodded in agreement. "How do we analyze root causes effectively?"

"Analyzing root causes effectively," Jim replied, "requires a methodical approach, using techniques such as the 5 Whys, fishbone diagrams, and fault tree analysis to identify underlying causes and contributing factors. We must also involve cross-functional teams and stakeholders in the analysis process to gain diverse perspectives and insights."

He continued to discuss the importance of root cause analysis techniques, emphasizing their role in driving continuous improvement and preventing recurrence of failures.

"As executives," Jim concluded, "it's essential for us to foster a culture of learning from mistakes. By creating a safe environment, analyzing root causes, and embracing failure as an opportunity for growth, we can build a resilient organization that thrives in the face of adversity."

After Jim's presentation concluded, the room buzzed with discussion as the team members exchanged ideas and insights. They now had a clearer understanding of learning from mistakes and were ready to apply this knowledge to their leadership roles within the company.

As the meeting adjourned, Jim felt a sense of optimism. With a solid grasp of mistake-learning principles, he knew that his team was better equipped to embrace failure as a stepping stone to success and drive the growth and innovation of Cartwright Industries into the future.

Chapter 6: Navigating Corporate Governance

Understanding Corporate Governance

I n the hushed boardroom of Cartwright Industries, Jim Cartwright, the CEO, stood at the head of the table, ready to lead his senior management team through the intricacies of corporate governance. This chapter, he knew, was vital for ensuring the company's ethical conduct, accountability, and long-term sustainability.

"Good morning, everyone," Jim began, his voice projecting authority and warmth. "Today, we embark on a journey to explore the cornerstone of corporate ethics and responsibility: corporate governance."

He clicked the remote, and the slide titled **Understanding Corporate Governance: Guiding Ethical Leadership** illuminated the screen.

"Let's start by understanding why corporate governance is crucial," Jim continued. "What role does it play in our organization and the broader business landscape?"

Paul Bennett, the COO, leaned forward. "Corporate governance provides the framework for how our company is directed and controlled, ensuring transparency, accountability, and ethical behavior. It defines the roles and responsibilities of the board, management, and shareholders, safeguarding the interests of all stakeholders."

Jim nodded, acknowledging Paul's insight. "Exactly. Now, let's delve into the principles of corporate governance."

He clicked to the next slide, which displayed **Principles of Corporate Governance**.

"The first principle," Jim explained, "is **Transparency**. This involves the clear and open disclosure of information to stakeholders, enabling them to make informed decisions and hold management accountable."

Janet Ross, the HR Director, raised a question. "How do we ensure transparency in our corporate governance practices?"

Jim appreciated Janet 's engagement. "Ensuring transparency involves adopting policies and practices that promote disclosure of financial, operational, and strategic information. It also requires effective communication with stakeholders through channels such as annual reports, shareholder meetings, and corporate websites."

He continued to elaborate on the importance of transparency in building trust and credibility with stakeholders.

"Next," Jim said, clicking to the next slide, "we have **Accountability**."

"Accountability," he explained, "involves holding individuals and entities responsible for their actions and decisions, ensuring that they act in the best interests of the company and its stakeholders."

Richard Shaw, the head of sales, nodded in agreement. "How do we promote accountability in our corporate governance structure?"

"Promoting accountability," Jim replied, "requires establishing clear lines of authority and responsibility, implementing checks and balances to prevent conflicts of interest, and holding individuals accountable for their performance and conduct."

He continued to discuss the importance of accountability mechanisms, such as performance evaluations, ethics codes, and whistleblower policies, in fostering a culture of accountability within the organization.

"As executives," Jim concluded, "it's essential for us to understand and uphold the principles of corporate governance. By embracing transparency, accountability, and ethical leadership, we can build a foundation of trust and integrity that drives the long-term success of Cartwright Industries."

After Jim's presentation concluded, the room buzzed with discussion as the team members exchanged ideas and insights. They now had a clearer understanding of corporate governance and its importance in guiding ethical leadership within the company.

As the meeting adjourned, Jim felt a sense of pride. With a solid grasp of corporate governance principles, he knew that his team was better equipped to navigate the complexities of corporate ethics and responsibility, ensuring the continued success and sustainability of Cartwright Industries.

Roles of the Board of Directors

Following the enlightening discussion on the principles of corporate governance, Jim Cartwright shifted the focus of the senior management team to another critical aspect: understanding the roles of the board of directors. He knew that a clear understanding of the board's responsibilities was essential for effective governance and strategic decision-making at Cartwright Industries.

"Good morning, everyone," Jim began, his voice carrying a tone of respect and authority. "Now, let's explore the pivotal roles played by the board of directors in shaping the direction and governance of our company."

He clicked the remote, and the slide titled **Roles of the Board of Directors: Guiding Corporate Strategy** illuminated the screen.

"Let's start by understanding the significance of the board's role," Jim continued. "What are the primary responsibilities entrusted to the board of directors?"

Paul Bennett, the COO, leaned forward. "The board of directors provides oversight, guidance, and strategic direction to the company. It is responsible for setting the company's strategic objectives, appointing and evaluating senior management, and ensuring that the company operates in compliance with legal and regulatory requirements."

Jim nodded, affirming Paul's insight. "Precisely. Now, let's delve deeper into the specific roles of the board."

He clicked to the next slide, which displayed **Key Roles of the Board of Directors**.

"The first role," Jim explained, "is **Strategic Oversight**. The board is responsible for setting the company's strategic direction, approving major strategic initiatives, and monitoring the implementation of strategic plans to ensure alignment with the company's mission and objectives."

Janet Ross, the HR Director, raised a question. "How does the board provide strategic oversight effectively?"

Jim appreciated Janet 's inquiry. "Providing strategic oversight involves actively engaging with management to review and evaluate strategic plans, assess risks and opportunities, and make informed decisions that drive the long-term success of the company."

He continued to elaborate on the importance of strategic alignment and decision-making processes within the board.

"Next," Jim said, clicking to the next slide, "we have **Executive Leadership**."

"Executive leadership," he explained, "involves appointing and evaluating the performance of senior management, including the CEO and other key executives. The board provides guidance, support, and mentorship to senior management, ensuring that they have the necessary resources and support to lead the company effectively."

Richard Shaw, the head of sales, nodded in agreement. "How does the board support executive leadership?"

"Supporting executive leadership," Jim replied, "involves establishing clear expectations, providing feedback and coaching, and holding senior management accountable for their performance and conduct. The board also plays a key role in succession planning, ensuring that the company has a strong pipeline of talent to fill key leadership positions."

He continued to discuss the importance of collaboration and communication between the board and senior management in driving organizational success.

"As executives," Jim concluded, "it's essential for us to understand and respect the roles of the board of directors. By working together effectively, we can leverage the board's expertise and guidance to navigate challenges, seize opportunities, and drive the success of Cartwright Industries."

After Jim's presentation concluded, the room buzzed with discussion as the team members exchanged ideas and insights. They now had a clearer understanding of the roles of the board of directors and its significance in guiding corporate strategy within the company.

As the meeting adjourned, Jim felt a sense of confidence. With a solid grasp of the board's responsibilities, he knew that his team was better equipped to collaborate effectively with the board and drive the strategic direction of Cartwright Industries for years to come.

Compliance and Ethical Standards

After an engaging discussion on the roles of the board of directors, Jim Cartwright directed the attention of the senior management team to another critical aspect: compliance and ethical standards. He knew that upholding integrity and adherence to regulations were essential for maintaining trust and credibility in Cartwright Industries.

"Good morning, everyone," Jim began, his voice carrying a tone of gravity and responsibility. "Now, let's delve into the paramount importance of compliance and ethical standards in our corporate governance framework."

He clicked the remote, and the slide titled **Compliance and Ethical Standards: Upholding Integrity** illuminated the screen.

"Let's start by understanding why compliance and ethical standards are non-negotiable," Jim continued. "What are the implications of failing to adhere to regulatory requirements and ethical principles?"

Paul Bennett, the COO, spoke up. "Compliance ensures that we operate within the boundaries of laws and regulations, mitigating legal risks and safeguarding the reputation of our company. Ethical standards, on the other hand, define our commitment to integrity, honesty, and responsible conduct, fostering trust among stakeholders and contributing to long-term sustainability."

Jim nodded, acknowledging Paul's astute observation. "Exactly. Now, let's explore the principles of compliance and ethical standards."

He clicked to the next slide, which displayed **Principles of Compliance and Ethical Standards**.

"The first principle," Jim explained, "is **Adherence to Laws and Regulations**. Compliance with applicable laws, regulations, and industry standards is fundamental to our operations and governance. It ensures that we conduct business ethically and responsibly, avoiding legal liabilities and reputational damage."

Janet Ross, the HR Director, raised a question. "How do we ensure compliance effectively?"

Jim appreciated Janet 's inquiry. "Ensuring compliance involves implementing robust policies, procedures, and controls to identify, assess, and mitigate legal and regulatory risks. We must also provide ongoing training and awareness programs to educate employees about their responsibilities and the importance of compliance."

He continued to elaborate on the importance of a proactive approach to compliance management, emphasizing the need for regular audits and reviews to monitor compliance effectiveness.

"Next," Jim said, clicking to the next slide, "we have **Ethical Conduct**."

"Ethical conduct," he explained, "involves adhering to principles of honesty, integrity, and fairness in all our business dealings. It requires us to act in the best interests of our stakeholders, including employees, customers, suppliers, and the community, and to uphold the highest standards of ethical behavior."

Richard Shaw, the head of sales, nodded in agreement. "How do we promote ethical conduct throughout the organization?"

"Promoting ethical conduct," Jim replied, "requires leadership commitment, clear communication of values, and leading by example. We must establish a culture where ethical behavior is celebrated and rewarded, and where employees feel empowered to speak up about ethical concerns without fear of retaliation."

He continued to discuss the importance of ethical leadership and accountability in fostering a culture of integrity within the organization.

"As executives," Jim concluded, "it's essential for us to prioritize compliance and ethical standards in our corporate governance practices. By upholding integrity, adhering to regulations, and promoting ethical conduct, we can build trust, credibility, and long-term success for Cartwright Industries."

After Jim's presentation concluded, the room buzzed with discussion as the team members exchanged ideas and insights. They now had a clearer understanding of compliance and ethical standards and their significance in maintaining the integrity and reputation of Cartwright Industries.

As the meeting adjourned, Jim felt a sense of assurance. With a solid commitment to compliance and ethics, he knew that his team was better equipped to navigate the complexities of corporate governance and uphold the values of Cartwright Industries for years to come.

Transparency and Accountability

With the weighty discussions on compliance and ethical standards behind them, Jim Cartwright redirected the focus of the senior management team to another pivotal aspect: transparency and accountability. He understood that these elements were the bedrock of trust and confidence in Cartwright Industries' governance structure.

"Good morning, everyone," Jim began, his tone resonating with conviction and sincerity. "Now, let's explore the critical importance of transparency and accountability in our corporate governance framework."

He clicked the remote, and the slide titled **Transparency and Accountability: Building Trust** illuminated the screen.

"Let's start by understanding why transparency and accountability are indispensable," Jim continued. "What are the ramifications of fostering a culture lacking in transparency and accountability?"

Paul Bennett, the COO, leaned forward, his expression serious. "Transparency ensures that our stakeholders have access to accurate and timely information about our company's performance, operations, and governance practices. Accountability, on the other hand, holds individuals and entities responsible for their actions and decisions, fostering trust and confidence in our leadership."

Jim nodded in agreement. "Precisely. Now, let's delve into the principles of transparency and accountability."

He clicked to the next slide, which displayed **Principles of Transparency and Accountability**.

"The first principle," Jim explained, "is **Open Communication**. Transparency requires clear and open communication with stakeholders, including shareholders, employees, customers, and regulators. It entails providing timely and accurate information about our company's activities, financial performance, and governance practices."

Janet Ross, the HR Director, raised a question. "How do we ensure open communication effectively?"

Jim appreciated Janet 's engagement. "Ensuring open communication involves establishing channels for dialogue and feedback, such as regular shareholder meetings, employee town halls, and customer feedback mechanisms. We must also be proactive in addressing stakeholder inquiries and concerns in a timely and transparent manner."

He continued to elaborate on the importance of fostering a culture of open communication to build trust and credibility with stakeholders.

"Next," Jim said, clicking to the next slide, "we have **Accountability Mechanisms**."

"Accountability mechanisms," he explained, "involve establishing processes and controls to hold individuals and entities accountable for their actions and decisions. It requires defining clear roles and responsibilities, setting performance expectations, and implementing mechanisms for monitoring and evaluating performance."

Richard Shaw, the head of sales, nodded in agreement. "How

do we implement accountability mechanisms effectively?"

"Implementing accountability mechanisms effectively," Jim replied, "requires a combination of leadership commitment, performance metrics, and consequences for non-compliance. We must establish a culture where accountability is valued and rewarded, and where individuals are held responsible for their conduct and performance."

He continued to discuss the importance of accountability mechanisms in driving transparency and fostering a culture of responsibility within the organization.

"As executives," Jim concluded, "it's essential for us to prioritize transparency and accountability in our corporate governance practices. By fostering open communication and implementing accountability mechanisms, we can build trust, confidence, and long-term success for Cartwright Industries."

After Jim's presentation concluded, the room buzzed with discussion as the team members exchanged ideas and insights. They now had a clearer understanding of transparency and accountability and their significance in maintaining trust and confidence in Cartwright Industries' governance structure.

As the meeting adjourned, Jim felt a sense of assurance. With a solid commitment to transparency and accountability, he knew that his team was better equipped to navigate the complexities of corporate governance and uphold the values of Cartwright Industries for years to come.

Managing Stakeholder Relationships

After the enlightening discussions on transparency and accountability, Jim Cartwright directed the attention of the senior management team to another crucial aspect: managing stakeholder relationships. He understood that nurturing positive relationships with stakeholders was essential for Cartwright Industries' reputation and long-term success.

"Good morning, everyone," Jim began, his tone warm yet resolute. "Now, let's explore the vital importance of managing stakeholder relationships in our corporate governance framework."

He clicked the remote, and the slide titled **Managing Stakeholder Relationships: Fostering Trust and Collaboration** illuminated the screen.

"Let's start by understanding why managing stakeholder relationships is paramount," Jim continued. "What are the benefits of fostering positive relationships with our stakeholders?"

Paul Bennett, the COO, spoke up. "Managing stakeholder relationships allows us to build trust, credibility, and goodwill with our stakeholders. It fosters collaboration, alignment of interests, and support for our business objectives, ultimately contributing to our long-term success and sustainability."

Jim nodded in agreement. "Precisely. Now, let's delve into the principles of managing stakeholder relationships."

He clicked to the next slide, which displayed **Principles of Managing Stakeholder Relationships**.

"The first principle," Jim explained, "is **Understanding Stakeholder Needs and Expectations**. Managing stakeholder relationships requires us to understand the needs, expectations, and concerns of our stakeholders, including shareholders, employees, customers, suppliers, and the community."

Janet Ross, the HR Director, raised a question. "How do we understand stakeholder needs effectively?"

Jim appreciated Janet 's inquiry. "Understanding stake-holder needs involves actively listening to their feedback, conducting surveys and focus groups, and engaging in dialogue to gain insights into their priorities and concerns. We must also consider the diverse interests and perspectives of our stakeholders and tailor our engagement strategies accordingly."

He continued to elaborate on the importance of empathy and responsiveness in managing stakeholder relationships.

"Next," Jim said, clicking to the next slide, "we have **Building Trust and Credibility**."

"Building trust and credibility," he explained, "is essential for fostering positive relationships with our stakeholders. It requires us to act with integrity, honesty, and transparency in all our interactions, delivering on our promises and commitments, and being accountable for our actions."

Richard Shaw, the head of sales, nodded in agreement. "How do we build trust and credibility effectively?"

"Building trust and credibility," Jim replied, "involves consistent communication, reliable performance, and demonstrating empathy and understanding towards our stakeholders. We must also be responsive to their needs and concerns, and seek to resolve issues and conflicts in a fair and transparent manner."

He continued to discuss the importance of trust-building strategies in managing stakeholder relationships effectively.

"As executives," Jim concluded, "it's essential for us to prioritize managing stakeholder relationships in our corporate governance practices. By understanding stakeholder needs, building trust and credibility, and fostering collaboration and alignment, we can build strong and resilient relationships that drive the success of Cartwright Industries."

After Jim's presentation concluded, the room buzzed with discussion as the team members exchanged ideas and insights. They now had a clearer understanding of managing stakeholder relationships and their significance in maintaining trust and confidence in Cartwright Industries' governance structure.

As the meeting adjourned, Jim felt a sense of optimism. With a solid commitment to managing stakeholder relationships, he knew that his team was better equipped to navigate the complexities of corporate governance and uphold the values of Cartwright Industries for years to come.

Governance Best Practices

Following the insightful discussions on managing stakeholder relationships, Jim Cartwright shifted the focus of the senior management team to another critical aspect: governance best practices. He understood that adopting best practices was essential for Cartwright Industries to operate efficiently, ethically, and in alignment with industry standards.

"Good morning, everyone," Jim began, his voice resonating with authority and determination. "Now, let's explore the importance of governance best practices in our corporate governance framework."

He clicked the remote, and the slide titled **Governance Best Practices: Driving Excellence** illuminated the screen.

"Let's start by understanding why governance best practices are indispensable," Jim continued. "What are the benefits of adopting best practices in our governance processes?"

Paul Bennett, the COO, spoke up. "Governance best practices provide guidelines and standards for effective decision-making, risk management, and accountability. They help us optimize our governance processes, enhance transparency and oversight, and mitigate risks, ultimately driving excellence and value creation for our stakeholders."

Jim nodded in agreement. "Precisely. Now, let's delve into the principles of governance best practices."

He clicked to the next slide, which displayed **Principles of Governance Best Practices**.

"The first principle," Jim explained, "is **Board Composition and Structure**. Governance best practices recommend that boards be composed of diverse, independent directors with relevant expertise and experience. Boards should also establish appropriate committees, such as audit, compensation, and nominating committees, to oversee key areas of governance."

Janet Ross, the HR Director, raised a question. "How do we ensure effective board composition and structure?"

Jim appreciated Janet 's inquiry. "Ensuring effective board composition and structure involves conducting regular board assessments to evaluate the skills, diversity, and independence of directors. Boards should also implement term limits and succession planning to refresh board membership and maintain continuity of leadership."

He continued to elaborate on the importance of board diversity and independence in driving effective governance.

"Next," Jim said, clicking to the next slide, "we have **Risk Management and Oversight**."

"Risk management and oversight," he explained, "are critical components of governance best practices. Boards should establish robust risk management processes and frameworks to identify, assess, and mitigate risks across all aspects of the business. They should also provide oversight of key risks and monitor the effectiveness of risk management activities."

Richard Shaw, the head of sales, nodded in agreement. "How do we enhance risk management and oversight?"

"Enhancing risk management and oversight," Jim replied, "involves integrating risk management into strategic planning and decision-making processes, ensuring that risks are considered at all levels of the organization. Boards should also receive regular reports on risk exposures and mitigation efforts, and engage with management to address emerging risks and opportunities."

He continued to discuss the importance of proactive risk management in safeguarding the interests of stakeholders.

"As executives," Jim concluded, "it's essential for us to prioritize governance best practices in our corporate governance framework. By adopting best practices in board composition, risk management, and oversight, we can enhance transparency, accountability, and value creation for Cartwright Industries."

After Jim's presentation concluded, the room buzzed with discussion as the team members exchanged ideas and insights. They now had a clearer understanding of governance best practices and their significance in driving excellence and value creation within the company.

As the meeting adjourned, Jim felt a sense of determination. With a solid commitment to governance best practices, he knew that his team was better equipped to navigate the complexities of corporate governance and lead Cartwright Industries to new heights of success and sustainability.

7

Chapter 7: Leading Through Change

The Dynamics of Organizational Change

As the sun rose over the horizon, casting its warm glow through the windows of the Cartwright Industries boardroom, Jim Cartwright gathered his senior management team for a crucial discussion on leading through change. He knew that in today's fast-paced business environment, adaptability and resilience were essential for success.

"Good morning, everyone," Jim began, his voice steady and reassuring. "Today, we embark on a journey to explore the dynamics of organizational change and how we, as leaders, can navigate through it successfully."

He clicked the remote, and the slide titled **The Dynamics of Organizational Change: Embracing Transformation** illuminated the screen.

"Let's start by understanding why organizational change is inevitable," Jim continued. "What are the forces driving change in our business environment?"

Paul Bennett, the COO, spoke up. "Organizational change is driven by a variety of factors, including technological advancements, market disruptions, competitive pressures, and shifts in consumer preferences. To remain competitive and sustainable, organizations must continuously adapt and evolve in response to these changes."

Jim nodded, acknowledging Paul's insight. "Exactly. Now, let's delve into the dynamics of organizational change."

He clicked to the next slide, which displayed **Key Dynamics of Organizational Change**.

"The first dynamic," Jim explained, "is **Disruption and Uncertainty**. Organizational change often disrupts the status quo, creating uncertainty and ambiguity for employees. Leaders must navigate through this uncertainty by providing clarity, direction, and support to their teams."

Janet Ross, the HR Director, raised a question. "How do we manage disruption and uncertainty effectively?"

Jim appreciated Janet 's inquiry. "Managing disruption and uncertainty involves effective communication, empathy, and resilience. Leaders must communicate transparently with their teams, acknowledging their concerns and providing reassurance about the path forward. They must also demonstrate resilience and adaptability, embracing change as an opportunity for growth and innovation."

He continued to elaborate on the importance of leadership during times of uncertainty, emphasizing the need for empathy and resilience in guiding teams through change.

"Next," Jim said, clicking to the next slide, "we have **Resistance and Acceptance**."

"Resistance and acceptance," he explained, "are common

reactions to organizational change. While some employees may resist change due to fear of the unknown or perceived loss of control, others may embrace it as an opportunity for growth and development. Leaders must understand these dynamics and proactively address resistance while fostering acceptance and buy-in."

Richard Shaw, the head of sales, nodded in agreement. "How do we foster acceptance and manage resistance?"

"Fostering acceptance and managing resistance," Jim replied, "involves engaging employees in the change process, soliciting their input and feedback, and addressing their concerns and objections. Leaders must also provide support and resources to help employees adapt to change, including training, coaching, and mentorship."

He continued to discuss the importance of empathy and communication in building trust and credibility during times of change.

"As executives," Jim concluded, "it's essential for us to understand the dynamics of organizational change and lead with empathy, resilience, and vision. By embracing change as an opportunity for growth and innovation, we can navigate through uncertainty and lead Cartwright Industries to new heights of success."

After Jim's presentation concluded, the room buzzed with discussion as the team members exchanged ideas and insights. They now had a clearer understanding of the dynamics of organizational change and their role as leaders in guiding Cartwright Industries through periods of transformation.

As the meeting adjourned, Jim felt a sense of optimism. With a solid commitment to leading through change, he knew that his team was better equipped to adapt, innovate, and thrive in an ever-evolving business landscape.

Communicating Change Effectively

With the foundation laid on understanding the dynamics of organizational change, Jim Cartwright transitioned the discussion to another critical aspect: communicating change effectively. He recognized that clear and transparent communication was essential for guiding employees through periods of transformation.

"Good morning, everyone," Jim began, his voice projecting confidence and empathy. "Now, let's explore the importance of communicating change effectively and how it can shape our journey through transformation."

He clicked the remote, and the slide titled **Communicating Change Effectively: Inspiring Confidence** illuminated the screen.

"Let's start by understanding why effective communication is crucial during times of change," Jim continued. "What role does communication play in guiding employees through transformation?"

Paul Bennett, the COO, spoke up. "Effective communication provides clarity, context, and direction to employees, helping them understand the reasons behind the change, the impact on their roles and responsibilities, and the desired outcomes. It inspires confidence, builds trust, and fosters commitment to the change process."

Jim nodded in agreement. "Precisely. Now, let's delve into the principles of communicating change effectively."

He clicked to the next slide, which displayed **Principles of Communicating Change**.

"The first principle," Jim explained, "is **Transparency and Openness**. Communicating change transparently involves sharing information openly and honestly with employees, including the reasons for the change, the expected impact, and the timeline for implementation. It requires leaders to be transparent about both the opportunities and challenges associated with the change."

Janet Ross, the HR Director, raised a question. "How do we ensure transparency and openness in our communication?"

Jim appreciated Janet's inquiry. "Ensuring transparency and openness involves regular communication through multiple channels, such as town hall meetings, email updates, and one-on-one discussions. Leaders must be accessible and approachable, encouraging employees to ask questions, express concerns, and provide feedback."

He continued to elaborate on the importance of two-way communication in building trust and credibility during times of change.

"Next," Jim said, clicking to the next slide, "we have **Clarity and Consistency**."

"Clarity and consistency," he explained, "are essential for ensuring that employees understand the change and its implications clearly. Communication should be clear, concise, and consistent across all channels and messages, avoiding jargon or ambiguity that may confuse or mislead employees."

Richard Shaw, the head of sales, nodded in agreement. "How do we achieve clarity and consistency in our communication?"

"Achieving clarity and consistency," Jim replied, "involves crafting clear and concise messages that highlight the key objectives, benefits, and expectations of the change. Leaders must also reinforce these messages consistently through repeated communication and alignment of actions with words."

He continued to discuss the importance of repetition and reinforcement in reinforcing key messages during times of change.

"As executives," Jim concluded, "it's essential for us to prioritize communicating change effectively to inspire confidence, build trust, and foster commitment among employees. By embracing transparency, clarity, and consistency in our communication, we can guide Cartwright Industries through transformation and towards a brighter future."

After Jim's presentation concluded, the room buzzed with discussion as the team members exchanged ideas and insights. They now had a clearer understanding of the principles of communicating change effectively and their role as leaders in guiding Cartwright Industries through periods of transformation.

As the meeting adjourned, Jim felt a sense of determination. With a solid commitment to communicating change effectively, he knew that his team was better equipped to navigate through uncertainty and lead Cartwright Industries to new heights of success.

Overcoming Resistance

As the discussion on communicating change effectively concluded, Jim Cartwright turned the attention of his senior management team to another critical aspect: overcoming resistance. He understood that resistance to change was natural but needed to be addressed proactively to ensure successful implementation.

"Good morning, everyone," Jim began, his voice firm yet

empathetic. "Now, let's explore the challenges of overcoming resistance during times of change and how we can navigate through it effectively."

He clicked the remote, and the slide titled **Overcoming Resistance: Embracing Transformation** illuminated the screen.

"Let's start by understanding why resistance to change occurs," Jim continued. "What are the common reasons why employees resist change?"

Paul Bennett, the COO, spoke up. "Resistance to change can stem from fear of the unknown, loss of control, uncertainty about the future, or perceived threats to one's job or status. It's essential for us to address these concerns and provide reassurance and support to employees as we navigate through change."

Jim nodded in agreement. "Precisely. Now, let's delve into the strategies for overcoming resistance."

He clicked to the next slide, which displayed **Strategies for Overcoming Resistance**.

"The first strategy," Jim explained, "is **Engagement and Involvement**. Involving employees in the change process empowers them to take ownership and become advocates for the change. Leaders must engage employees by soliciting their input, addressing their concerns, and involving them in decision-making to foster a sense of ownership and commitment."

Janet Ross, the HR Director, raised a question. "How do we effectively engage and involve employees in the change process?"

Jim appreciated Janet 's inquiry. "Effectively engaging and involving employees involves creating opportunities for dialogue, collaboration, and participation. Leaders must communicate openly about the reasons for the change, its objectives, and the expected outcomes, and invite employees to share their ideas, feedback, and concerns."

He continued to elaborate on the importance of empowering employees to become champions of change through active engagement and involvement.

"Next," Jim said, clicking to the next slide, "we have **Education and Training**."

"Education and training," he explained, "are essential for helping employees adapt to change and acquire the skills and knowledge needed for success in the new environment. Leaders must provide comprehensive training programs, resources, and support to help employees develop the competencies required to thrive in the changing landscape."

Richard Shaw, the head of sales, nodded in agreement. "How do we ensure effective education and training?"

"Ensuring effective education and training," Jim replied, "involves assessing the needs of employees, designing tailored training programs, and providing ongoing support and feedback. Leaders must also communicate the benefits of training and provide incentives to encourage participation and commitment."

He continued to discuss the importance of investing in employee development to facilitate successful change implementation.

"As executives," Jim concluded, "it's essential for us to prioritize overcoming resistance by engaging, involving, educating, and empowering our employees. By addressing their concerns and providing support and resources, we can navigate through resistance and lead Cartwright Industries towards a brighter future."

After Jim's presentation concluded, the room buzzed with discussion as the team members exchanged ideas and insights. They now had a clearer understanding of the strategies for overcoming resistance and their role as leaders in guiding Cartwright Industries through periods of transformation.

As the meeting adjourned, Jim felt a sense of determination. With a solid commitment to overcoming resistance, he knew that his team was better equipped to navigate through challenges and lead Cartwright Industries to new heights of success and innovation.

Change Management Models

With the discussion on overcoming resistance concluded, Jim Cartwright directed the focus of his senior management team to another crucial aspect: change management models. He recognized the importance of having structured frameworks to guide the organization through the complexities of change.

"Good morning, everyone," Jim began, his tone resolute yet adaptable. "Now, let's explore the significance of change management models in navigating through transformation and how they can shape our approach to change."

He clicked the remote, and the slide titled **Change Management Models: Guiding Transformation** illuminated the screen.

"Let's start by understanding why change management models are essential," Jim continued. "What role do these models play in facilitating successful change?"

Paul Bennett, the COO, spoke up. "Change management models provide structured frameworks and methodologies for planning, implementing, and monitoring change initiatives. They help us identify the drivers of change, assess the impact on the organization, and develop strategies to mitigate risks and maximize opportunities."

Jim nodded in agreement. "Precisely. Now, let's delve into the principles of change management models."

He clicked to the next slide, which displayed **Principles of Change Management Models**.

"The first principle," Jim explained, "is **Diagnosis and Assessment**. Change management models emphasize the importance of diagnosing the need for change and assessing the readiness and capacity of the organization to adapt. This involves conducting thorough analyses of the current state, identifying gaps and challenges, and aligning the change initiative with strategic objectives."

Janet Ross, the HR Director, raised a question. "How do we effectively diagnose and assess the need for change?"

Jim appreciated Janet's inquiry. "Effectively diagnosing and assessing the need for change involves engaging stakeholders, conducting surveys and assessments, and gathering data to understand the root causes of the issues or opportunities driving the change. It also requires evaluating the organization's culture, capabilities, and resources to determine its readiness for change."

He continued to elaborate on the importance of thorough diagnosis and assessment in laying the groundwork for successful change management.

"Next," Jim said, clicking to the next slide, "we have **Planning and Strategy**."

"Planning and strategy," he explained, "are essential components of change management models. They involve developing comprehensive plans and strategies to guide the implementation of change initiatives, including defining objectives, timelines, roles, and responsibilities. Leaders must ensure alignment between the change initiative and the organization's overall strategy to maximize impact and minimize disruption."

Richard Shaw, the head of sales, nodded in agreement. "How do we develop effective plans and strategies?"

"Developing effective plans and strategies," Jim replied, "involves engaging cross-functional teams, leveraging best practices and benchmarks, and soliciting input from key stakeholders. Leaders must also anticipate potential challenges and develop contingency plans to address them proactively."

He continued to discuss the importance of strategic planning and alignment in driving successful change initiatives.

"As executives," Jim concluded, "it's essential for us to leverage change management models to guide our approach to change effectively. By diagnosing the need for change, developing comprehensive plans and strategies, and aligning the change initiative with strategic objectives, we can navigate through transformation with confidence and purpose."

After Jim's presentation concluded, the room buzzed with discussion as the team members exchanged ideas and insights. They now had a clearer understanding of change management models and their role in guiding Cartwright Industries through periods of transformation.

As the meeting adjourned, Jim felt a sense of optimism. With a solid commitment to leveraging change management models, he knew that his team was better equipped to navigate through change and lead Cartwright Industries to new heights of success and innovation.

Sustaining Change

Following the insightful discussion on change management models, Jim Cartwright turned the focus of the senior management team to another critical aspect: sustaining change. He understood that the true measure of success lay in the organization's ability to embed change into its culture and operations for long-term impact.

"Good morning, everyone," Jim began, his voice projecting determination and foresight. "Now, let's explore the challenges of sustaining change and how we can ensure that our efforts lead to lasting transformation."

He clicked the remote, and the slide titled **Sustaining Change: Embedding Transformation** illuminated the screen.

"Let's start by understanding why sustaining change is essential," Jim continued. "What are the benefits of ensuring that our efforts lead to lasting transformation?"

Paul Bennett, the COO, spoke up. "Sustaining change ensures that the benefits of transformation are realized over the long term, driving continuous improvement, innovation, and growth. It fosters a culture of adaptability and resilience, positioning the organization for success in an ever-evolving business landscape."

Jim nodded in agreement. "Precisely. Now, let's delve into the strategies for sustaining change."

He clicked to the next slide, which displayed **Strategies for Sustaining Change**.

"The first strategy," Jim explained, "is **Leadership Commitment and Alignment**. Sustaining change requires ongoing leadership commitment and alignment at all levels of the organization. Leaders must continue to champion the change, communicate its importance, and lead by example to ensure that it remains a priority."

Janet Ross, the HR Director, raised a question. "How do we maintain leadership commitment and alignment over the long term?"

Jim appreciated Janet 's inquiry. "Maintaining leadership commitment and alignment involves embedding change into the organization's vision, values, and strategic objectives. Leaders must integrate change initiatives into performance metrics, incentives, and recognition programs to reinforce their importance and ensure accountability."

He continued to elaborate on the importance of sustained leadership engagement in driving lasting transformation.

"Next," Jim said, clicking to the next slide, "we have **Culture and Communication**."

"Culture and communication," he explained, "are critical enablers of sustained change. Leaders must cultivate a culture that embraces change, innovation, and continuous improvement, fostering openness, collaboration, and agility. Communication plays a key role in reinforcing the change narrative, celebrating successes, and addressing challenges openly and transparently."

Richard Shaw, the head of sales, nodded in agreement. "How do we foster a culture that sustains change?"

"Fostering a culture that sustains change," Jim replied, "involves modeling the desired behaviors, recognizing and rewarding innovation and adaptability, and providing ongoing support and resources for learning and development. Leaders must also encourage feedback and empower employees to contribute to the change process."

He continued to discuss the importance of culture and communication in embedding change into the fabric of the organization.

"As executives," Jim concluded, "it's essential for us to prioritize sustaining change by maintaining leadership commitment, fostering a culture of innovation, and communicating openly and transparently. By embedding change into our culture and operations, we can ensure that our efforts lead to lasting transformation and continued success for Cartwright Industries."

After Jim's presentation concluded, the room buzzed with discussion as the team members exchanged ideas and insights. They now had a clearer understanding of the strategies for sustaining change and their role as leaders in driving lasting transformation within the organization.

As the meeting adjourned, Jim felt a sense of confidence. With a solid commitment to sustaining change, he knew that his team was better equipped to navigate through challenges and lead Cartwright Industries towards a future of continued growth and innovation.

Evaluating Change Impact

With the discussion on sustaining change concluded, Jim Cartwright turned the attention of his senior management team to another crucial aspect: evaluating change impact. He understood that assessing the effectiveness of change initiatives was essential for continuous improvement and informed decision-making.

"Good morning, everyone," Jim began, his voice firm yet receptive. "Now, let's explore the importance of evaluating change impact and how it can inform our future strategies and actions."

He clicked the remote, and the slide titled **Evaluating Change Impact: Informing Decision-Making** illuminated the screen.

"Let's start by understanding why evaluating change impact is essential," Jim continued. "What insights can we gain from assessing the effectiveness of our change initiatives?"

Paul Bennett, the COO, spoke up. "Evaluating change impact allows us to measure the success of our initiatives, identify areas for improvement, and learn from our experiences. It provides valuable insights into the outcomes of change, the challenges encountered, and the lessons learned, enabling us to refine our strategies and approaches in the future."

Jim nodded in agreement. "Precisely. Now, let's delve into the strategies for evaluating change impact."

He clicked to the next slide, which displayed **Strategies for Evaluating Change Impact**.

"The first strategy," Jim explained, "is **Defining Key Performance Indicators (KPIs)**. Evaluating change impact begins with defining clear and measurable KPIs that align with the objectives of the change initiative. These KPIs serve as benchmarks for assessing progress, tracking performance, and measuring success."

Janet Ross, the HR Director, raised a question. "How do we define effective KPIs for evaluating change impact?"

Jim appreciated Janet 's inquiry. "Defining effective KPIs involves identifying relevant metrics that capture the desired outcomes of the change initiative, such as productivity improvements, cost savings, customer satisfaction, or employee engagement. These KPIs should be specific, measurable, achievable, relevant, and time-bound (SMART), providing actionable insights into the impact of change."

He continued to elaborate on the importance of selecting the right KPIs to measure the success of change initiatives accurately.

"Next," Jim said, clicking to the next slide, "we have **Data Collection and Analysis.**"

"Data collection and analysis," he explained, "are essential for evaluating change impact objectively and systematically. Leaders must collect data from multiple sources, such as performance reports, employee surveys, customer feedback, and financial statements, and analyze it to assess the outcomes and effectiveness of change initiatives."

Richard Shaw, the head of sales, nodded in agreement. "How do we ensure effective data collection and analysis?"

"Ensuring effective data collection and analysis," Jim replied, "involves establishing robust data collection processes, leveraging technology and analytics tools, and engaging experts to interpret the findings. Leaders must also triangulate data from multiple sources to validate insights and identify correlations, trends, and patterns."

He continued to discuss the importance of data-driven decision-making in evaluating change impact.

"As executives," Jim concluded, "it's essential for us to prioritize evaluating change impact to inform our decision-making and drive continuous improvement. By defining KPIs, collecting and analyzing data, and leveraging insights to refine our strategies, we can ensure that our change initiatives lead to meaningful outcomes and sustainable success for Cartwright Industries."

After Jim's presentation concluded, the room buzzed with

discussion as the team members exchanged ideas and insights. They now had a clearer understanding of the strategies for evaluating change impact and their role as leaders in driving continuous improvement within the organization.

As the meeting adjourned, Jim felt a sense of anticipation. With a solid commitment to evaluating change impact, he knew that his team was better equipped to learn from their experiences and drive future success for Cartwright Industries.

8

Chapter 8: Innovation and Growth

Fostering an Innovative Culture

As the morning sun cast a warm glow into the Cartwright Industries boardroom, Jim Cartwright gathered his senior management team for a crucial discussion on innovation and growth. He understood that fostering an innovative culture was essential for driving sustainable growth and staying ahead in a competitive market.

"Good morning, everyone," Jim began, his voice brimming with energy and enthusiasm. "Today, we embark on a journey to explore the importance of innovation and growth, starting with the critical aspect of fostering an innovative culture."

He clicked the remote, and the slide titled **Fostering an Innovative Culture: Igniting Creativity** illuminated the screen.

"Let's start by understanding why fostering an innovative culture is essential," Jim continued. "What are the benefits of nurturing a culture of innovation within our organization?"

Paul Bennett, the COO, spoke up. "Fostering an innovative culture encourages creativity, experimentation, and risk-taking among employees. It drives continuous improvement, drives new ideas and solutions, and fosters a spirit of entrepreneurship and agility, positioning the organization for long-term growth and success."

Jim nodded in agreement. "Precisely. Now, let's delve into the strategies for fostering an innovative culture."

He clicked to the next slide, which displayed **Strategies for Fostering an Innovative Culture**.

"The first strategy," Jim explained, "is **Empowering Employees**. Fostering an innovative culture begins with empowering employees to explore new ideas, take calculated risks, and challenge the status quo. Leaders must create an environment that encourages autonomy, creativity, and ownership, empowering employees to innovate and experiment without fear of failure."

Janet Ross, the HR Director, raised a question. "How do we empower employees to be more innovative?"

Jim appreciated Janet 's inquiry. "Empowering employees involves providing them with the autonomy, resources, and support they need to pursue their ideas and initiatives. Leaders must encourage open communication, recognize and reward innovative behavior, and provide opportunities for learning and development."

He continued to elaborate on the importance of empowering employees as drivers of innovation within the organization.

"Next," Jim said, clicking to the next slide, "we have **Encouraging Collaboration**."

"Encouraging collaboration," he explained, "is another key

aspect of fostering an innovative culture. Innovation thrives in an environment where diverse perspectives are valued, and ideas are freely shared and refined through collaboration. Leaders must create opportunities for cross-functional collaboration, brainstorming sessions, and idea exchanges to spark creativity and innovation."

Richard Shaw, the head of sales, nodded in agreement. "How do we encourage collaboration effectively?"

"Encouraging collaboration effectively," Jim replied, "involves breaking down silos, promoting open communication channels, and facilitating team-building activities that foster trust and camaraderie. Leaders must also lead by example, actively participating in collaborative efforts and valuing diverse viewpoints."

He continued to discuss the importance of collaboration in driving innovation and growth within the organization.

"As executives," Jim concluded, "it's essential for us to prioritize fostering an innovative culture to drive sustainable growth and success. By empowering employees, encouraging collaboration, and embracing a mindset of continuous learning and improvement, we can unleash the full potential of our organization and lead Cartwright Industries to new heights of innovation and growth."

After Jim's presentation concluded, the room buzzed with excitement as the team members exchanged ideas and insights. They now had a clearer understanding of the strategies for fostering an innovative culture and their role as leaders in driving innovation and growth within the organization.

As the meeting adjourned, Jim felt a sense of anticipation. With a solid commitment to fostering an innovative culture, he knew that his team was poised to unleash their creativity and drive meaningful change within Cartwright Industries.

Identifying Growth Opportunities

With the foundation laid on fostering an innovative culture, Jim Cartwright continued the discussion with his senior management team on the critical aspect of identifying growth opportunities. He knew that identifying and capitalizing on growth opportunities was essential for sustaining momentum and driving long-term success.

"Good morning, everyone," Jim began, his voice resonating with anticipation. "Now, let's explore the importance of identifying growth opportunities and how we can uncover new avenues for innovation and expansion."

He clicked the remote, and the slide titled **Identifying Growth Opportunities: Unlocking Potential** illuminated the screen.

"Let's start by understanding why identifying growth opportunities is essential," Jim continued. "What benefits can we gain from uncovering new avenues for growth within our organization?"

Paul Bennett, the COO, spoke up. "Identifying growth opportunities allows us to capitalize on market trends, customer needs, and emerging technologies, driving innovation and expansion. It enables us to diversify our revenue streams, enter new markets, and stay ahead of competitors, positioning the organization for sustainable growth and success."

Jim nodded in agreement. "Precisely. Now, let's delve into the strategies for identifying growth opportunities."

He clicked to the next slide, which displayed **Strategies for Identifying Growth Opportunities**.

"The first strategy," Jim explained, "is **Market Research and Analysis**. Identifying growth opportunities begins with conducting comprehensive market research and analysis to understand market trends, customer preferences, and competitive dynamics. Leaders must gather data, analyze market trends, and identify gaps or unmet needs that present opportunities for innovation and growth."

Janet Ross, the HR Director, raised a question. "How do we conduct effective market research and analysis?"

Jim appreciated Janet 's inquiry. "Conducting effective market research and analysis involves leveraging data analytics, customer feedback, and industry insights to gain a deep understanding of market dynamics. Leaders must also monitor competitor activities, track emerging technologies, and anticipate future trends to identify potential growth opportunities proactively."

He continued to elaborate on the importance of staying informed and proactive in identifying growth opportunities.

"Next," Jim said, clicking to the next slide, "we have **Collaborative Ideation**."

"Collaborative ideation," he explained, "involves engaging employees, customers, and other stakeholders in the process of generating and refining ideas for growth. Leaders must create opportunities for brainstorming sessions, innovation workshops, and idea challenges to harness the collective creativity and insights of the organization."

Richard Shaw, the head of sales, nodded in agreement. "How do we facilitate collaborative ideation effectively?"

"Facilitating collaborative ideation effectively," Jim replied, "involves creating a supportive environment where all ideas are welcomed and valued. Leaders must encourage participation, foster a culture of openness and creativity, and provide resources and support to bring ideas to fruition."

He continued to discuss the importance of collaboration in uncovering innovative growth opportunities.

"As executives," Jim concluded, "it's essential for us to prioritize identifying growth opportunities to drive innovation and expansion within our organization. By conducting market research, fostering collaborative ideation, and staying informed and proactive, we can uncover new avenues for growth and lead Cartwright Industries to new heights of success."

After Jim's presentation concluded, the room buzzed with excitement as the team members exchanged ideas and insights. They now had a clearer understanding of the strategies for identifying growth opportunities and their role as leaders in driving innovation and growth within the organization.

As the meeting adjourned, Jim felt a sense of optimism. With a solid commitment to identifying growth opportunities, he knew that his team was well-positioned to unlock new avenues for innovation and expansion within Cartwright Industries.

Investing in R&D

Following the discussion on identifying growth opportunities, Jim Cartwright transitioned the focus of his senior management team to another critical aspect: investing in Research and Development (R&D). He understood that R&D investment was vital for fueling innovation and driving sustainable growth in a rapidly evolving market landscape.

"Good morning, everyone," Jim began, his voice infused

with determination and foresight. "Now, let's explore the importance of investing in Research and Development (R&D) and how it can drive innovation and growth within our organization."

He clicked the remote, and the slide titled **Investing in R&D: Nurturing Innovation** illuminated the screen.

"Let's start by understanding why investing in R&D is essential," Jim continued. "What role does R&D play in fostering innovation and driving sustainable growth?"

Paul Bennett, the COO, spoke up. "Investing in R&D allows us to explore new technologies, develop innovative products and services, and stay ahead of market trends. It fosters a culture of experimentation and learning, driving continuous improvement and positioning the organization for long-term success and competitiveness."

Jim nodded in agreement. "Precisely. Now, let's delve into the strategies for investing in R&D."

He clicked to the next slide, which displayed **Strategies for Investing in R&D**.

"The first strategy," Jim explained, "is **Resource Allocation**. Investing in R&D begins with allocating sufficient resources, including funding, talent, and infrastructure, to support innovation initiatives. Leaders must prioritize R&D investments, aligning them with strategic objectives and allocating resources effectively to drive maximum impact."

Janet Ross, the HR Director, raised a question. "How do we allocate resources effectively for R&D?"

Jim appreciated Janet 's inquiry. "Allocating resources effectively for R&D involves setting clear priorities, conducting cost-benefit analyses, and balancing short-term and long-term investments. Leaders must also foster a culture of accountability and transparency, ensuring that R&D investments are aligned with strategic goals and deliver measurable results."

He continued to elaborate on the importance of strategic resource allocation in driving successful R&D initiatives.

"Next," Jim said, clicking to the next slide, "we have **Collaboration and Partnerships**."

"Collaboration and partnerships," he explained, "are essential for leveraging external expertise, resources, and networks to enhance R&D capabilities. Leaders must seek opportunities for collaboration with industry partners, research institutions, and startups to access new ideas, technologies, and markets."

Richard Shaw, the head of sales, nodded in agreement. "How do we foster collaboration and partnerships effectively?"

"Fostering collaboration and partnerships effectively," Jim replied, "involves building strategic relationships, fostering trust and mutual benefit, and establishing clear communication channels. Leaders must also cultivate a culture of openness and collaboration within the organization, encouraging cross-functional teamwork and knowledge sharing."

He continued to discuss the importance of collaboration in driving innovation and growth through R&D.

"As executives," Jim concluded, "it's essential for us to prioritize investing in R&D to drive innovation and growth within our organization. By allocating resources effectively, fostering collaboration and partnerships, and embracing a culture of experimentation and learning, we can unlock new opportunities for innovation and lead Cartwright Industries to new heights of success."

After Jim's presentation concluded, the room buzzed with excitement as the team members exchanged ideas and insights. They now had a clearer understanding of the strategies for investing in R&D and their role as leaders in driving innovation and growth within the organization.

As the meeting adjourned, Jim felt a sense of determination. With a solid commitment to investing in R&D, he knew that his team was well-equipped to pioneer breakthrough innovations and propel Cartwright Industries into a future of continued growth and success.

Managing Innovation Projects

Building upon the discussion of investing in Research and Development (R&D), Jim Cartwright guided his senior management team's focus towards another crucial aspect: managing innovation projects. He understood that effective project management was essential for translating R&D investments into tangible outcomes and driving organizational growth.

"Good morning, everyone," Jim began, his voice projecting assurance and focus. "Now, let's delve into the importance of managing innovation projects and how it can accelerate our journey towards growth and success."

He clicked the remote, and the slide titled **Managing Innovation Projects: Turning Ideas into Reality** illuminated the screen.

"Let's start by understanding why managing innovation projects is crucial," Jim continued. "What role does effective project management play in realizing the potential of our R&D investments?"

Paul Bennett, the COO, spoke up. "Managing innovation projects ensures that R&D investments are translated into tangible outcomes, such as new products, services, or processes. It involves planning, execution, and monitoring of projects to deliver results on time, within budget, and according to specifications. Effective project management drives efficiency, accountability, and alignment, maximizing the impact of our innovation initiatives."

Jim nodded in agreement. "Precisely. Now, let's explore the strategies for managing innovation projects."

He clicked to the next slide, which displayed **Strategies for Managing Innovation Projects**.

"The first strategy," Jim explained, "is **Project Planning and Execution**. Managing innovation projects begins with comprehensive planning and execution to define project objectives, scope, timelines, and deliverables. Leaders must establish clear project plans, allocate resources effectively, and monitor progress closely to ensure that projects stay on track and meet expectations."

Janet Ross, the HR Director, raised a question. "How do we ensure effective project planning and execution?"

Jim appreciated Janet 's inquiry. "Ensuring effective project planning and execution involves engaging stakeholders, setting realistic goals and milestones, and mitigating risks proactively. Leaders must also foster a culture of collaboration and accountability, empowering project teams to take ownership of their work and adapt to changes as needed."

He continued to elaborate on the importance of proactive planning and execution in driving successful innovation projects.

"Next," Jim said, clicking to the next slide, "we have **Cross-Functional Collaboration**."

"Cross-functional collaboration," he explained, "is essential for integrating diverse perspectives, expertise, and resources into innovation projects. Leaders must facilitate collaboration between different departments, teams, and stakeholders to leverage their collective knowledge and capabilities. Cross-functional collaboration fosters creativity, problem-solving, and innovation, driving project success and organizational growth."

Richard Shaw, the head of sales, nodded in agreement. "How do we promote cross-functional collaboration effectively?"

"Promoting cross-functional collaboration effectively," Jim replied, "involves creating opportunities for interdisciplinary teamwork, fostering open communication channels, and breaking down silos between departments. Leaders must also provide incentives, recognition, and support for collaborative efforts, encouraging employees to collaborate and share knowledge freely."

He continued to discuss the importance of collaboration in driving successful innovation projects.

"As executives," Jim concluded, "it's essential for us to prioritize managing innovation projects to maximize the impact of our R&D investments. By planning and executing projects effectively, fostering cross-functional collaboration, and empowering project teams, we can accelerate innovation and drive sustainable growth within Cartwright Industries."

After Jim's presentation concluded, the room buzzed with enthusiasm as the team members exchanged ideas and insights. They now had a clearer understanding of the strategies for managing innovation projects and their role as leaders in driving project success and organizational growth within the company.

As the meeting adjourned, Jim felt a sense of confidence. With a solid commitment to managing innovation projects, he knew that his team was well-equipped to transform ideas into reality and propel Cartwright Industries towards a future of continued innovation and success.

Scaling Successful Innovations

Following the insightful discussion on managing innovation projects, Jim Cartwright directed the focus of his senior management team to another critical aspect: scaling successful innovations. He understood that scaling successful innovations was essential for maximizing their impact and driving widespread organizational growth.

"Good morning, everyone," Jim began, his voice resonating with determination and foresight. "Now, let's explore the importance of scaling successful innovations and how it can accelerate our journey towards growth and success."

He clicked the remote, and the slide titled **Scaling Successful Innovations: Amplifying Impact** illuminated the screen.

"Let's start by understanding why scaling successful innovations is crucial," Jim continued. "What benefits can we gain from expanding the reach of our successful innovations within our organization?"

Paul Bennett, the COO, spoke up. "Scaling successful innovations allows us to amplify their impact, drive widespread adoption, and generate significant returns on investment. It enables us to leverage proven solutions, processes, or business models to drive efficiency, growth, and competitiveness across the organization."

Jim nodded in agreement. "Precisely. Now, let's delve into the strategies for scaling successful innovations."

He clicked to the next slide, which displayed **Strategies for**

Scaling Successful Innovations.

"The first strategy," Jim explained, "is **Standardization and Replication**. Scaling successful innovations begins with standardizing processes, systems, or products to enable replication across different parts of the organization. Leaders must identify best practices, document procedures, and develop standardized templates or tools to facilitate replication and ensure consistency."

Janet Ross, the HR Director, raised a question. "How do we standardize and replicate successful innovations effectively?"

Jim appreciated Janet 's inquiry. "Standardizing and replicating successful innovations effectively involves creating clear guidelines, providing training and support, and fostering a culture of continuous improvement. Leaders must also establish feedback mechanisms to capture lessons learned and refine processes iteratively."

He continued to elaborate on the importance of standardization and replication in scaling successful innovations.

"Next," Jim said, clicking to the next slide, "we have **Resource Allocation and Investment**."

"Resource allocation and investment," he explained, "are essential for scaling successful innovations by providing the necessary funding, talent, and infrastructure to support expansion efforts. Leaders must allocate resources strategically, prioritizing investments that maximize the impact of successful innovations and drive sustainable growth."

Richard Shaw, the head of sales, nodded in agreement. "How do we allocate resources effectively for scaling successful innovations?"

"Allocating resources effectively for scaling successful innovations," Jim replied, "involves conducting cost-benefit analyses, assessing scalability and potential returns on investment, and aligning resources with strategic priorities. Leaders must also monitor and evaluate the performance of scaled initiatives, adjusting resource allocation as needed to optimize outcomes."

He continued to discuss the importance of strategic resource allocation in scaling successful innovations.

"As executives," Jim concluded, "it's essential for us to prioritize scaling successful innovations to drive widespread impact and growth within our organization. By standardizing and replicating best practices, allocating resources strategically, and fostering a culture of continuous improvement, we can leverage our successes to propel Cartwright Industries to new heights of innovation and success."

After Jim's presentation concluded, the room buzzed with enthusiasm as the team members exchanged ideas and insights. They now had a clearer understanding of the strategies for scaling successful innovations and their role as leaders in driving organizational growth within the company.

As the meeting adjourned, Jim felt a sense of determination. With a solid commitment to scaling successful innovations, he knew that his team was well-equipped to expand the reach of their successes and drive meaningful change within Cartwright Industries.

Innovation Metrics and KPIs

As the discussion on scaling successful innovations concluded, Jim Cartwright shifted the focus of his senior management team to another critical aspect: innovation metrics and Key Performance Indicators (KPIs). He understood that measuring innovation performance was essential for tracking progress, identifying areas for improvement, and driving continuous innovation and growth.

"Good morning, everyone," Jim began, his voice filled with anticipation and purpose. "Now, let's explore the importance of innovation metrics and KPIs and how they can drive our journey towards growth and success."

He clicked the remote, and the slide titled **Innovation Metrics and KPIs: Tracking Progress** illuminated the screen.

"Let's start by understanding why innovation metrics and KPIs are crucial," Jim continued. "What role do they play in driving innovation and growth within our organization?"

Paul Bennett, the COO, spoke up. "Innovation metrics and KPIs allow us to measure the effectiveness of our innovation efforts, track progress towards goals, and identify areas for optimization. They provide valuable insights into the outcomes of innovation initiatives, the performance of innovation teams, and the overall health of our innovation ecosystem."

Jim nodded in agreement. "Precisely. Now, let's delve into the strategies for defining innovation metrics and KPIs."

He clicked to the next slide, which displayed **Strategies for Defining Innovation Metrics and KPIs**.

"The first strategy," Jim explained, "is **Alignment with Strategic Objectives**. Defining innovation metrics and KPIs begins with aligning them with our strategic goals and objectives. Leaders must identify key areas of focus, such as product innovation, process improvement, or market expansion, and develop metrics and KPIs that measure progress towards these goals."

Janet Ross, the HR Director, raised a question. "How do

we ensure alignment with strategic objectives when defining innovation metrics and KPIs?"

Jim appreciated Janet 's inquiry. "Ensuring alignment with strategic objectives involves engaging stakeholders, clarifying expectations, and establishing clear linkages between innovation metrics and broader organizational goals. Leaders must also communicate the rationale behind selected metrics and KPIs, ensuring buy-in and alignment across the organization."

He continued to elaborate on the importance of alignment in driving effective innovation measurement.

"Next," Jim said, clicking to the next slide, "we have **Measurable and Actionable Metrics**."

"Measurable and actionable metrics," he explained, "are essential for providing clear and meaningful insights into innovation performance. Leaders must develop metrics and KPIs that are quantifiable, relevant, and actionable, allowing teams to track progress, identify trends, and make data-driven decisions to drive continuous improvement."

Richard Shaw, the head of sales, nodded in agreement. "How do we ensure that our metrics are both measurable and actionable?"

"Ensuring that our metrics are both measurable and actionable," Jim replied, "involves defining clear measurement criteria, setting achievable targets, and establishing processes for collecting, analyzing, and reporting data. Leaders must also provide teams with the tools and resources needed to interpret metrics effectively and take corrective actions as needed."

He continued to discuss the importance of developing actionable metrics for driving innovation and growth.

"As executives," Jim concluded, "it's essential for us to

prioritize defining innovation metrics and KPIs to drive our innovation efforts and achieve our strategic objectives. By aligning metrics with strategic goals, ensuring measurability and actionability, and fostering a culture of data-driven decision-making, we can maximize the impact of our innovation initiatives and lead Cartwright Industries to new heights of success."

After Jim's presentation concluded, the room buzzed with enthusiasm as the team members exchanged ideas and insights. They now had a clearer understanding of the importance of innovation metrics and KPIs in driving organizational growth and their role as leaders in driving innovation within the company.

As the meeting adjourned, Jim felt a sense of satisfaction. With a solid commitment to defining innovation metrics and KPIs, he knew that his team was well-equipped to track progress, identify opportunities, and drive continuous innovation and growth within Cartwright Industries.

Chapter 9: Risk Management

Identifying Potential Risks

As the morning light filtered through the windows of the Cartwright Industries boardroom, Jim Cartwright gathered his senior management team for a crucial discussion on risk management. He understood that identifying potential risks was the first step towards safeguarding the organization's interests and ensuring long-term success in a volatile business landscape.

"Good morning, everyone," Jim began, his voice carrying authority and concern. "Today, we embark on a journey to explore the importance of risk management and how it can protect our organization from potential threats."

He clicked the remote, and the slide titled **Identifying Potential Risks: Safeguarding Our Future** illuminated the screen.

"Let's start by understanding why identifying potential risks is crucial," Jim continued. "What threats could jeopardize our organization's operations, reputation, or financial stability?"

Paul Bennett, the COO, spoke up. "Identifying potential risks allows us to anticipate and mitigate threats before they escalate into crises. It involves assessing internal and external factors, such as market volatility, regulatory changes, cybersecurity threats, or supply chain disruptions, that could impact our organization's ability to achieve its objectives."

Jim nodded in agreement. "Precisely. Now, let's delve into the strategies for identifying potential risks."

He clicked to the next slide, which displayed **Strategies for Identifying Potential Risks**.

"The first strategy," Jim explained, "is **Comprehensive Risk Assessment**. Identifying potential risks begins with conducting a comprehensive risk assessment to evaluate the likelihood and potential impact of various threats on our organization. Leaders must analyze internal processes, external factors, and industry trends to identify vulnerabilities and emerging risks."

Janet Ross, the HR Director, raised a question. "How do we conduct a comprehensive risk assessment effectively?"

Jim appreciated Janet 's inquiry. "Conducting a comprehensive risk assessment effectively involves engaging stakeholders, leveraging expertise from different departments, and utilizing risk management frameworks and tools. Leaders must also gather data, conduct risk workshops, and prioritize risks based on their severity and likelihood of occurrence."

He continued to elaborate on the importance of thorough risk assessment in safeguarding the organization's interests.

"Next," Jim said, clicking to the next slide, "we have **Scenario Planning**."

"Scenario planning," he explained, "involves developing

hypothetical scenarios to anticipate and prepare for potential risks and their consequences. Leaders must identify various scenarios, such as economic downturns, natural disasters, or technological failures, and assess their potential impact on our organization's operations, assets, and stakeholders."

Richard Shaw, the head of sales, nodded in agreement. "How do we develop effective scenario plans?"

"Developing effective scenario plans," Jim replied, "involves conducting scenario workshops, engaging subject matter experts, and analyzing historical data to inform scenario development. Leaders must also consider different risk scenarios and their likelihood of occurrence, developing response strategies and contingency plans to mitigate potential impacts."

He continued to discuss the importance of scenario planning in risk management.

"As executives," Jim concluded, "it's essential for us to prioritize identifying potential risks to protect our organization from threats and ensure long-term success. By conducting comprehensive risk assessments, engaging in scenario planning, and fostering a culture of risk awareness, we can proactively mitigate potential risks and safeguard the future of Cartwright Industries."

After Jim's presentation concluded, the room buzzed with focused energy as the team members exchanged insights and perspectives on identifying potential risks. They now had a clearer understanding of the importance of risk management and their role in protecting the organization's interests.

As the meeting adjourned, Jim felt a sense of confidence. With a solid commitment to identifying potential risks, he knew that his team was well-prepared to navigate challenges of the key risk assessment techniques."

He clicked to the next slide, which displayed **Key Risk Assessment Techniques**.

"The first technique," Jim explained, "is **Quantitative Risk Analysis**. This technique involves using numerical data and statistical methods to assess the probability and magnitude of potential risks. Leaders utilize quantitative models, such as probabilistic risk assessment or Monte Carlo simulations, to quantify risk exposure and prioritize mitigation efforts based on quantitative metrics."

Janet Ross, the HR Director, raised a question. "How do we conduct quantitative risk analysis effectively?"

Jim appreciated Janet 's inquiry. "Conducting quantitative risk analysis effectively involves collecting relevant data, identifying key risk indicators, and applying statistical techniques to analyze risk scenarios. Leaders must also interpret the results of quantitative analysis in the context of organizational objectives and risk tolerance, informing decision-making and risk management strategies."

He continued to elaborate on the importance of quantitative risk analysis in gaining insights into potential risks.

"Next," Jim said, clicking to the next slide, "we have **Qualitative Risk Assessment**."

"Qualitative risk assessment," he explained, "involves evaluating potential risks based on subjective judgments and expert opinions. Leaders utilize qualitative methods, such as risk matrices, risk registers, or risk workshops, to identify and assess risks qualitatively based on factors such as severity, likelihood, and impact on organizational objectives."

Richard Shaw, the head of sales, nodded in agreement. "How do we conduct qualitative risk assessment effectively?"

Developing a Risk Management Plan

Having explored the techniques for identifying and assessing potential risks, Jim Cartwright led his senior management team towards the crucial next step in risk management: developing a comprehensive risk management plan. He understood that a well-defined plan was essential for effectively mitigating risks and ensuring the resilience of Cartwright Industries in the face of uncertainties.

"Good morning, everyone," Jim began, his voice resonating with purpose and clarity. "Now, let's transition our focus to the development of a risk management plan and how it can fortify our organization against potential threats."

He clicked the remote, and the slide titled **Developing a Risk Management Plan: Safeguarding Our Future** illuminated the screen.

"Let's start by understanding why developing a risk management plan is imperative," Jim continued. "How can a structured plan help us mitigate potential risks and protect our organization's interests?"

Paul Bennett, the COO, spoke up. "A risk management plan provides a roadmap for identifying, assessing, and mitigating risks systematically. It outlines the strategies, processes, and resources required to manage risks effectively, ensuring that our organization remains resilient and adaptive in the face of uncertainties."

Jim nodded in agreement. "Exactly. Now, let's delve into the key components of a risk management plan."

He clicked to the next slide, which displayed **Key Components of a Risk Management Plan**.

"The first component," Jim explained, "is **Risk Identifica-**

tion and Assessment. This involves identifying potential risks, assessing their likelihood and potential impact, and prioritizing them based on their severity and relevance to organizational objectives. Leaders must utilize insights from risk assessments to inform decision-making and develop targeted mitigation strategies."

Janet Ross, the HR Director, raised a question. "How do we effectively identify and assess risks for inclusion in the plan?"

Jim appreciated Janet 's inquiry. "Effectively identifying and assessing risks involves engaging stakeholders, leveraging diverse perspectives, and utilizing risk assessment techniques, such as quantitative and qualitative analysis. Leaders must also consider internal and external factors, emerging trends, and historical data to ensure comprehensive coverage of potential risks."

He continued to elaborate on the importance of thorough risk identification and assessment in developing a robust risk management plan.

"Next," Jim said, clicking to the next slide, "we have **Risk Mitigation Strategies**."

"Risk mitigation strategies," he explained, "involve developing proactive measures to reduce the likelihood or impact of potential risks. Leaders must identify appropriate risk mitigation measures, such as risk avoidance, risk transfer, risk reduction, or risk acceptance, based on the nature and severity of identified risks. Mitigation strategies should be aligned with organizational objectives and risk tolerance levels."

Richard Shaw, the head of sales, nodded in agreement. "How do we determine the most effective risk mitigation strategies?"

"Determining the most effective risk mitigation strategies," Jim replied, "involves conducting cost-benefit analyses, assessing feasibility and resource requirements, and considering the potential effectiveness of different approaches. Leaders must also prioritize mitigation efforts based on the severity and likelihood of identified risks, focusing resources on high-priority risks with the greatest potential impact."

He continued to discuss the importance of developing targeted risk mitigation strategies in reducing organizational vulnerabilities.

"As executives," Jim concluded, "it's essential for us to develop a comprehensive risk management plan to protect our organization from potential threats and ensure long-term resilience and success. By identifying and assessing risks, developing targeted mitigation strategies, and fostering a culture of risk awareness and accountability, we can fortify Cartwright Industries against uncertainties and safeguard its future."

After Jim's presentation concluded, the room buzzed with focused energy as the team members exchanged ideas and insights on developing a risk management plan. They now had a clearer understanding of the importance of proactive risk mitigation and their role in ensuring the resilience of Cartwright Industries.

As the meeting adjourned, Jim felt a sense of confidence. With a solid commitment to developing a comprehensive risk management plan, he knew that his team was well-prepared to navigate uncertainties and steer Cartwright Industries towards continued success and sustainability.

Mitigating and Managing Risks

With the framework for risk management plan laid out, Jim Cartwright directed his senior management team's focus towards the crucial aspect of mitigating and managing risks effectively. He understood that proactive measures were essential for minimizing the impact of potential threats and ensuring the resilience of Cartwright Industries.

"Good morning, everyone," Jim began, his voice projecting determination and readiness. "Now, let's delve into the strategies for mitigating and managing risks, and how they can safeguard our organization's interests in the face of uncertainties."

He clicked the remote, and the slide titled **Mitigating and Managing Risks: Building Resilience** illuminated the screen.

"Let's start by understanding why mitigating and managing risks is crucial," Jim continued. "How can proactive measures help us minimize the impact of potential threats and ensure the continuity of our operations?"

Paul Bennett, the COO, spoke up. "Mitigating and managing risks allows us to implement proactive measures to reduce the likelihood or impact of potential threats. By identifying and addressing vulnerabilities, implementing controls and safeguards, and developing response plans, we can enhance our organization's resilience and adaptability in the face of uncertainties."

Jim nodded in agreement. "Exactly. Now, let's explore the strategies for mitigating and managing risks."

He clicked to the next slide, which displayed **Strategies for Mitigating and Managing Risks**.

"The first strategy," Jim explained, "is **Risk Avoidance**. This involves taking actions to eliminate or avoid potential risks altogether. Leaders must identify high-risk activities, processes, or investments and develop alternative approaches or contingency plans to mitigate the risk of adverse outcomes."

Janet Ross, the HR Director, raised a question. "How do we effectively implement risk avoidance strategies?"

Jim appreciated Janet 's inquiry. "Effectively implementing risk avoidance strategies involves conducting thorough risk assessments, identifying root causes of potential risks, and developing alternative courses of action to mitigate them. Leaders must also communicate the rationale behind risk avoidance decisions and ensure alignment with organizational objectives and risk tolerance levels."

He continued to elaborate on the importance of proactive risk avoidance in minimizing organizational vulnerabilities.

"Next," Jim said, clicking to the next slide, "we have **Risk Transfer**."

"Risk transfer," he explained, "involves shifting the financial or operational burden of potential risks to external parties, such as insurance providers or contractual partners. Leaders must assess the feasibility and cost-effectiveness of risk transfer options, negotiate favorable terms and conditions, and ensure adequate coverage to mitigate the financial impact of potential losses."

Richard Shaw, the head of sales, nodded in agreement. "How do we determine the most appropriate risk transfer strategies?"

"Determining the most appropriate risk transfer strategies," Jim replied, "involves evaluating the nature and severity of potential risks, assessing available risk transfer mechanisms, and considering the organization's risk appetite and financial capabilities. Leaders must also monitor and review risk transfer arrangements regularly to ensure continued effectiveness and alignment with evolving business needs."

He continued to discuss the importance of risk transfer in diversifying risk exposure and protecting organizational assets.

"As executives," Jim concluded, "it's essential for us to implement proactive measures to mitigate and manage risks effectively, safeguarding the continuity and resilience of Cartwright Industries. By adopting risk avoidance and risk transfer strategies, and developing robust response plans, we can enhance our organization's ability to withstand uncertainties and emerge stronger from adversity."

After Jim's presentation concluded, the room buzzed with focused energy as the team members exchanged ideas and insights on mitigating and managing risks. They now had a clearer understanding of the importance of proactive risk management and their role in ensuring the resilience of Cartwright Industries.

As the meeting adjourned, Jim felt a sense of assurance. With a solid commitment to implementing proactive risk mitigation strategies, he knew that his team was well-prepared to navigate uncertainties and steer Cartwright Industries towards continued success and sustainability.

Crisis Management and Contingency Planning

As the discussion on mitigating and managing risks unfolded, Jim Cartwright guided his senior management team towards the critical aspect of crisis management and contingency planning. He understood that preparing for potential crises was essential for maintaining business continuity and protecting the reputation of Cartwright Industries in times of adversity.

"Good morning, everyone," Jim began, his voice infused with a sense of urgency and preparedness. "Now, let's shift our focus to crisis management and contingency planning, and how they can ensure the resilience of our organization in the face of unexpected challenges."

He clicked the remote, and the slide titled **Crisis Management and Contingency Planning: Ensuring Business Continuity** illuminated the screen.

"Let's start by understanding why crisis management and contingency planning are crucial," Jim continued. "How can proactive measures help us effectively respond to unexpected crises and ensure the continuity of our operations?"

Paul Bennett, the COO, spoke up. "Crisis management and contingency planning allow us to prepare for potential emergencies, such as natural disasters, supply chain disruptions, or cybersecurity breaches. By developing response strategies, establishing communication protocols, and identifying alternative resources and facilities, we can minimize the impact of crises and maintain business continuity."

Jim nodded in agreement. "Exactly. Now, let's explore the strategies for crisis management and contingency planning."

He clicked to the next slide, which displayed **Strategies for Crisis Management and Contingency Planning**.

"The first strategy," Jim explained, "is **Risk Assessment and Scenario Planning**. This involves conducting thorough risk assessments to identify potential crisis scenarios and developing response plans to address them. Leaders must anticipate various crisis scenarios, assess their potential impact on organizational operations, and formulate proactive strategies to mitigate risks and ensure preparedness."

Janet Ross, the HR Director, raised a question. "How do we conduct effective risk assessments and scenario planning for crisis management?"

Jim appreciated Janet 's inquiry. "Conducting effective risk assessments and scenario planning involves engaging stakeholders, leveraging diverse perspectives, and considering different crisis scenarios and their potential implications. Leaders must also simulate crisis scenarios through tabletop exercises or simulations to test response plans, identify gaps, and refine strategies."

He continued to elaborate on the importance of proactive risk assessment and scenario planning in crisis preparedness.

"Next," Jim said, clicking to the next slide, "we have **Communication and Coordination**."

"Communication and coordination," he explained, "are essential for ensuring effective crisis response and management. Leaders must establish clear communication channels, designate crisis management teams, and define roles and responsibilities to facilitate timely and coordinated responses to crises. Effective communication with stakeholders, including employees, customers, suppliers, and the media, is critical for maintaining trust and confidence during times of uncertainty."

Richard Shaw, the head of sales, nodded in agreement. "How do we ensure effective communication and coordination during crises?"

"Ensuring effective communication and coordination during crises," Jim replied, "involves developing communication protocols, conducting training and drills, and establishing backup communication systems to ensure redundancy and resilence. Leaders must also provide regular updates and transparent information to stakeholders, demonstrating proactive crisis management and commitment to resolution."

He continued to discuss the importance of communication and coordination in crisis response and management.

"As executives," Jim concluded, "it's essential for us to prioritize crisis management and contingency planning to ensure the resilience and continuity of Cartwright Industries. By conducting thorough risk assessments, developing proactive response plans, and fostering effective communication and coordination, we can navigate crises effectively and emerge stronger from adversity."

After Jim's presentation concluded, the room buzzed with focused energy as the team members exchanged ideas and insights on crisis management and contingency planning. They now had a clearer understanding of the importance of proactive preparedness and their role in safeguarding the continuity of Cartwright Industries.

As the meeting adjourned, Jim felt a sense of assurance. With a solid commitment to crisis management and contingency planning, he knew that his team was well-prepared to navigate uncertainties and steer Cartwright Industries towards continued success and resilience.

Learning from Past Crises

As the discussion on crisis management and contingency planning progressed, Jim Cartwright directed his senior management team's attention towards the crucial aspect of learning from past crises. He understood that analyzing past experiences was essential for identifying lessons learned and refining future crisis management strategies to ensure the resilience of Cartwright Industries.

"Good morning, everyone," Jim began, his voice resonating with reflection and insight. "Now, let's explore the importance of learning from past crises and how it can inform our future crisis management strategies."

He clicked the remote, and the slide titled **Learning from Past Crises: Strengthening Resilience** illuminated the screen.

"Let's start by understanding why learning from past crises is crucial," Jim continued. "How can analyzing past experiences help us identify lessons learned and refine our crisis management strategies?"

Paul Bennett, the COO, spoke up. "Learning from past crises allows us to identify strengths, weaknesses, and areas for improvement in our crisis management processes. By analyzing past incidents, assessing our response effectiveness, and identifying root causes of failures or successes, we can refine our crisis management strategies and enhance our organization's resilience to future crises."

Jim nodded in agreement. "Exactly. Now, let's explore the strategies for learning from past crises."

He clicked to the next slide, which displayed **Strategies for Learning from Past Crises**.

"The first strategy," Jim explained, "is **Post-Crisis Review and Evaluation**. This involves conducting thorough reviews and evaluations of past crisis incidents to assess response effectiveness, identify gaps in crisis management processes, and capture lessons learned. Leaders must engage stakeholders, including crisis management teams, frontline responders, and external partners, to gather diverse perspectives and insights."

Janet Ross, the HR Director, raised a question. "How do we conduct effective post-crisis reviews and evaluations?"

Jim appreciated Janet 's inquiry. "Conducting effective post-crisis reviews and evaluations involves establishing review committees, documenting incident timelines and actions taken, and conducting interviews or surveys to gather feedback from stakeholders. Leaders must also analyze root causes of failures or successes, identify areas for improvement, and develop actionable recommendations to enhance future crisis response."

He continued to elaborate on the importance of thorough post-crisis reviews in capturing lessons learned.

"Next," Jim said, clicking to the next slide, "we have **Continuous Improvement and Training**."

"Continuous improvement and training," he explained, "are essential for embedding lessons learned from past crises into our organizational culture and practices. Leaders must develop training programs, conduct tabletop exercises, and simulate crisis scenarios to reinforce best practices, build resilience, and enhance response readiness across the organization."

Richard Shaw, the head of sales, nodded in agreement. "How do we ensure ongoing learning and development in crisis management?"

"Ensuring ongoing learning and development in crisis management," Jim replied, "involves fostering a culture of continuous improvement, accountability, and adaptability. Leaders must provide resources and support for training and development initiatives, encourage knowledge sharing and collaboration, and recognize and reward proactive crisis management behaviors."

He continued to discuss the importance of continuous improvement and training in strengthening crisis management capabilities.

"As executives," Jim concluded, "it's essential for us to prioritize learning from past crises to inform and refine our future crisis management strategies. By conducting thorough post-crisis reviews, embracing continuous improvement, and investing in training and development, we can strengthen the resilience of Cartwright Industries and navigate future uncertainties with confidence."

After Jim's presentation concluded, the room buzzed with focused energy as the team members exchanged ideas and insights on learning from past crises. They now had a clearer understanding of the importance of reflection and continuous improvement in crisis management and their role in ensuring the resilience of Cartwright Industries.

As the meeting adjourned, Jim felt a sense of optimism. With a solid commitment to learning from past crises, he knew that his team was well-prepared to navigate uncertainties and steer Cartwright Industries towards continued success and resilience.

10

Chapter 10: Enhancing Operational Efficiency

Process Improvement Methods

As the need for operational efficiency became increasingly apparent, Jim Cartwright gathered his senior management team to explore strategies for enhancing operational efficiency, starting with process improvement methods. He knew that streamlining processes was essential for optimizing performance and driving sustainable growth for Cartwright Industries.

"Good morning, everyone," Jim began, his voice imbued with a sense of purpose and determination. "Today, we embark on a journey to enhance our operational efficiency, starting with an exploration of process improvement methods and how they can propel our organization towards greater success."

He clicked the remote, and the slide titled **Process Improvement Methods: Streamlining Operations** illuminated the screen.

"Let's begin by understanding why process improvement methods are crucial," Jim continued. "How can optimizing our processes help us achieve operational excellence and deliver greater value to our customers?"

Paul Bennett, the COO, spoke up. "Process improvement methods allow us to identify inefficiencies, eliminate waste, and streamline workflows to enhance productivity and quality. By optimizing our processes, we can reduce costs, shorten cycle times, and improve customer satisfaction, positioning Cartwright Industries for sustainable growth and competitive advantage."

Jim nodded in agreement. "Exactly. Now, let's explore the strategies for process improvement."

He clicked to the next slide, which displayed **Strategies for Process Improvement**.

"The first strategy," Jim explained, "is **Lean Six Sigma**. This methodology combines the principles of Lean and Six Sigma to identify and eliminate process inefficiencies, defects, and variation. Leaders must engage cross-functional teams, map current processes, and analyze data to identify areas for improvement and implement targeted solutions."

Janet Ross, the HR Director, raised a question. "How do we effectively implement Lean Six Sigma?"

Jim appreciated Janet 's inquiry. "Effectively implementing Lean Six Sigma involves providing training and resources for employees, empowering them to identify and implement process improvements. Leaders must also establish performance metrics, such as cycle time reduction or defect rate improvement, to measure progress and ensure alignment with organizational objectives."

He continued to elaborate on the importance of Lean Six Sigma in driving continuous improvement.

"Next," Jim said, clicking to the next slide, "we have **Business Process Reengineering**."

"Business Process Reengineering," he explained, "involves redesigning core business processes to achieve dramatic improvements in performance, such as cost reduction or cycle time reduction. Leaders must challenge existing assumptions, rethink workflows, and leverage technology and automation to streamline processes and drive innovation."

Richard Shaw, the head of sales, nodded in agreement. "How do we ensure successful business process reengineering?"

"Ensuring successful business process reengineering," Jim replied, "involves engaging stakeholders, including employees and customers, throughout the redesign process to gather insights and ensure alignment with their needs and expectations. Leaders must also communicate the rationale behind changes, manage resistance to change effectively, and monitor implementation progress to drive sustainable results."

He continued to discuss the importance of business process reengineering in driving transformative change.

"As executives," Jim concluded, "it's essential for us to embrace process improvement methods to enhance our operational efficiency and drive sustainable growth for Cartwright Industries. By adopting Lean Six Sigma and business process reengineering, and fostering a culture of continuous improvement and innovation, we can streamline our operations and deliver greater value to our customers."

After Jim's presentation concluded, the room buzzed with focused energy as the team members exchanged ideas and insights on process improvement methods. They now had a clearer understanding of the importance of optimizing processes and their role in driving operational excellence for Cartwright Industries.

As the meeting adjourned, Jim felt a sense of optimism. With a solid commitment to process improvement, he knew that his team was well-equipped to streamline operations and propel Cartwright Industries towards greater success and efficiency.

Lean and Six Sigma Principles

With the foundation of process improvement methods laid out, Jim Cartwright led his senior management team deeper into the realm of operational efficiency, focusing specifically on the principles of Lean and Six Sigma. He knew that embracing these principles was essential for driving continuous improvement and maximizing value for Cartwright Industries and its stakeholders.

"Good morning, everyone," Jim began, his voice projecting enthusiasm and determination. "Now, let's delve into the principles of Lean and Six Sigma and how they can guide us towards operational excellence and sustainable growth."

He clicked the remote, and the slide titled **Lean and Six Sigma Principles: Driving Efficiency** illuminated the screen.

"Let's start by understanding why Lean and Six Sigma principles are crucial," Jim continued. "How can embracing these principles help us optimize our processes and deliver greater value to our customers?"

Paul Bennett, the COO, spoke up. "Lean principles focus on eliminating waste and maximizing value by streamlining processes and minimizing non-value-added activities. Six

Sigma principles aim to reduce variation and defects in processes, ensuring consistency and quality in our products and services. By embracing Lean and Six Sigma, we can drive efficiency, quality, and customer satisfaction across our organization."

Jim nodded in agreement. "Exactly. Now, let's explore the key principles of Lean and Six Sigma."

He clicked to the next slide, which displayed **Key Principles of Lean and Six Sigma**.

"The first principle," Jim explained, "is **Identifying Value**. This involves understanding customer needs and preferences and identifying activities that directly contribute to meeting those needs. Leaders must engage with customers, map value streams, and distinguish between value-added and non-value-added activities to prioritize improvement efforts."

Janet Ross, the HR Director, raised a question. "How do we effectively identify value in our processes?"

Jim appreciated Janet 's inquiry. "Effectively identifying value involves engaging stakeholders, including customers and frontline employees, to gain insights into their expectations and requirements. Leaders must also analyze process flows, eliminate activities that do not add value, and focus resources on activities that directly contribute to meeting customer needs and organizational objectives."

He continued to elaborate on the importance of identifying value in driving process improvement.

"Next," Jim said, clicking to the next slide, "we have **Eliminating Waste**."

"Eliminating waste," he explained, "involves identifying and eliminating non-value-added activities, such as overproduction, waiting, or defects, that consume resources without contributing to customer value. Leaders must conduct waste walks, engage employees in continuous improvement initiatives, and implement visual management techniques to identify and eliminate waste systematically."

Richard Shaw, the head of sales, nodded in agreement. "How do we ensure successful waste elimination?"

"Ensuring successful waste elimination," Jim replied, "involves creating a culture of continuous improvement and empowerment, where employees are encouraged to identify and eliminate waste in their work processes. Leaders must provide training and resources for employees, recognize and reward improvement efforts, and monitor progress to sustain momentum and drive results."

He continued to discuss the importance of waste elimination in optimizing operational efficiency.

"As executives," Jim concluded, "it's essential for us to embrace Lean and Six Sigma principles to drive continuous improvement and deliver greater value to our customers. By identifying value, eliminating waste, and fostering a culture of continuous improvement, we can optimize our processes and achieve operational excellence for Cartwright Industries."

After Jim's presentation concluded, the room buzzed with focused energy as the team members exchanged ideas and insights on Lean and Six Sigma principles. They now had a clearer understanding of the importance of embracing these principles and their role in driving operational excellence for Cartwright Industries.

As the meeting adjourned, Jim felt a sense of excitement. With a solid commitment to Lean and Six Sigma principles, he knew that his team was well-equipped to optimize processes and deliver greater value for Cartwright Industries and its stakeholders.

Technology and Automation

As the discussion on operational efficiency continued, Jim Cartwright directed his senior management team's attention towards the transformative power of technology and automation. He knew that leveraging innovative technologies was essential for streamlining processes and driving sustainable growth for Cartwright Industries in the digital age.

"Good morning, everyone," Jim began, his voice infused with enthusiasm and forward-thinking. "Today, let's explore the role of technology and automation in enhancing our operational efficiency and driving innovation across Cartwright Industries."

He clicked the remote, and the slide titled **Technology and Automation: Driving Efficiency** illuminated the screen.

"Let's start by understanding why technology and automation are crucial," Jim continued. "How can leveraging innovative technologies help us optimize our processes and deliver greater value to our customers?"

Paul Bennett, the COO, spoke up. "Technology and automation enable us to streamline workflows, reduce manual effort, and increase productivity by automating repetitive tasks and integrating systems. By leveraging data analytics, artificial intelligence, and robotics, we can enhance decision-making, improve efficiency, and drive innovation across our organization."

Jim nodded in agreement. "Exactly. Now, let's explore the strategies for leveraging technology and automation."

He clicked to the next slide, which displayed **Strategies for**

Technology and Automation.

"The first strategy," Jim explained, "is **Process Digitization**. This involves digitizing manual processes and paperwork to streamline workflows, reduce errors, and improve accessibility and collaboration. Leaders must identify opportunities for digitization, invest in digital tools and platforms, and ensure seamless integration with existing systems and processes."

Janet Ross, the HR Director, raised a question. "How do we ensure successful process digitization?"

Jim appreciated Janet 's inquiry. "Ensuring successful process digitization involves engaging stakeholders, including frontline employees and IT professionals, to understand their needs and requirements. Leaders must provide training and support for employees transitioning to digital workflows, monitor adoption and usage, and iterate based on feedback to drive continuous improvement."

He continued to elaborate on the importance of process digitization in driving efficiency.

"Next," Jim said, clicking to the next slide, "we have **Automation of Routine Tasks**."

"Automation of routine tasks," he explained, "involves deploying robotic process automation (RPA) and other automation technologies to streamline repetitive tasks and eliminate manual effort. Leaders must identify opportunities for automation, assess feasibility and ROI, and develop a roadmap for implementation to maximize efficiency gains."

Richard Shaw, the head of sales, nodded in agreement. "How do we ensure successful automation of routine tasks?"

"Ensuring successful automation of routine tasks," Jim replied, "involves collaborating with cross-functional teams to identify automation opportunities and prioritize initiatives based on their potential impact on efficiency and effectiveness. Leaders must also address employee concerns and provide training and support for upskilling and reskilling to ensure successful adoption and integration of automation technologies."

He continued to discuss the importance of automation in driving productivity and innovation.

"As executives," Jim concluded, "it's essential for us to leverage technology and automation to optimize our processes and drive innovation across Cartwright Industries. By embracing process digitization and automation of routine tasks, and fostering a culture of innovation and collaboration, we can achieve operational excellence and deliver greater value to our customers."

After Jim's presentation concluded, the room buzzed with excitement as the team members exchanged ideas and insights on leveraging technology and automation. They now had a clearer understanding of the transformative potential of technology and their role in driving operational efficiency for Cartwright Industries.

As the meeting adjourned, Jim felt a sense of optimism. With a solid commitment to technology and automation, he knew that his team was well-positioned to harness the power of innovation and drive sustainable growth for Cartwright Industries in the digital age.

Measuring Operational Performance

As the discussion on operational efficiency progressed, Jim Cartwright led his senior management team towards the critical aspect of measuring operational performance. He knew that effectively measuring performance was essential for monitoring progress, identifying areas for improvement, and driving continuous enhancement of processes at Cartwright Industries.

"Good morning, everyone," Jim began, his voice infused with a sense of purpose and analytical insight. "Now, let's explore the importance of measuring operational performance and how it can guide us towards achieving our efficiency goals."

He clicked the remote, and the slide titled **Measuring Operational Performance: Monitoring Progress** illuminated the screen.

"Let's start by understanding why measuring operational performance is crucial," Jim continued. "How can effectively measuring performance help us track progress and identify opportunities for improvement?"

Paul Bennett, the COO, spoke up. "Measuring operational performance allows us to assess the effectiveness and efficiency of our processes, identify bottlenecks or areas of inefficiency, and track progress towards achieving organizational goals. By establishing key performance indicators (KPIs) and benchmarks, we can monitor performance trends, identify deviations from targets, and take corrective actions to drive continuous improvement."

Jim nodded in agreement. "Exactly. Now, let's explore the strategies for measuring operational performance."

He clicked to the next slide, which displayed **Strategies for Measuring Operational Performance**.

"The first strategy," Jim explained, "is **Establishing Key Performance Indicators (KPIs)**. This involves defining measurable metrics and targets that align with organizational objectives and strategic priorities. Leaders must engage stakeholders, including frontline employees and department heads, to identify relevant KPIs, establish baseline performance levels, and set achievable targets for improvement."

Janet Ross, the HR Director, raised a question. "How do we ensure that our KPIs are meaningful and actionable?"

Jim appreciated Janet 's inquiry. "Ensuring meaningful and actionable KPIs involves selecting metrics that are directly linked to organizational goals and have a clear cause-and-effect relationship with performance outcomes. Leaders must also ensure that KPIs are specific, measurable, achievable, relevant, and time-bound (SMART), and regularly review and revise them based on changing business needs and priorities."

He continued to elaborate on the importance of establishing KPIs in driving performance measurement.

"Next," Jim said, clicking to the next slide, "we have **Performance Dashboards and Scorecards**."

"Performance dashboards and scorecards," he explained, "provide visual representations of key performance metrics and trends, allowing stakeholders to monitor progress and make data-driven decisions. Leaders must design dashboards that provide actionable insights, facilitate drill-down analysis, and enable real-time tracking of performance against targets."

Richard Shaw, the head of sales, nodded in agreement. "How do we ensure that our performance dashboards are effective?"

"Ensuring effective performance dashboards," Jim replied, "involves designing user-friendly interfaces, prioritizing key metrics, and providing context and interpretation for the data presented. Leaders must also ensure data accuracy and reliability, establish data governance policies, and provide training and support for stakeholders to effectively utilize performance dashboards for decision-making."

He continued to discuss the importance of performance dashboards in providing visibility and transparency into operational performance.

"As executives," Jim concluded, "it's essential for us to establish robust measurement systems to monitor operational performance and drive continuous improvement. By defining meaningful KPIs, implementing performance dashboards, and fostering a culture of accountability and data-driven decision-making, we can optimize our processes and achieve operational excellence for Cartwright Industries."

After Jim's presentation concluded, the room buzzed with focused energy as the team members exchanged ideas and insights on measuring operational performance. They now had a clearer understanding of the importance of performance measurement and their role in driving continuous improvement for Cartwright Industries.

As the meeting adjourned, Jim felt a sense of satisfaction. With a solid commitment to measuring operational performance, he knew that his team was well-equipped to monitor progress, identify opportunities for improvement, and drive sustainable growth for Cartwright Industries.

Cost Efficiency Strategies

As the discussion on operational efficiency unfolded, Jim Cartwright steered his senior management team towards the critical aspect of implementing cost efficiency strategies. He understood that optimizing costs was essential for maintaining competitiveness and driving profitability for Cartwright Industries in a dynamic business environment.

"Good morning, everyone," Jim began, his voice reflecting a

blend of pragmatism and strategic foresight. "Now, let's delve into the importance of implementing cost efficiency strategies and how they can contribute to our overall operational excellence."

He clicked the remote, and the slide titled **Cost Efficiency Strategies: Maximizing Value** illuminated the screen.

"Let's start by understanding why cost efficiency strategies are crucial," Jim continued. "How can optimizing costs help us improve our bottom line and strengthen our competitive position?"

Paul Bennett, the COO, spoke up. "Implementing cost efficiency strategies allows us to maximize value for our stakeholders by reducing unnecessary expenses, optimizing resource allocation, and enhancing overall profitability. By identifying opportunities to streamline processes, negotiate favorable terms with suppliers, and eliminate waste, we can improve our cost structure and achieve sustainable growth."

Jim nodded in agreement. "Exactly. Now, let's explore the strategies for implementing cost efficiency."

He clicked to the next slide, which displayed **Strategies for Cost Efficiency**.

"The first strategy," Jim explained, "is **Process Optimization**. This involves analyzing existing processes to identify inefficiencies, streamline workflows, and reduce operating costs. Leaders must engage cross-functional teams, conduct value stream mapping, and prioritize improvement initiatives based on their potential impact on cost reduction and performance enhancement."

Janet Ross, the HR Director, raised a question. "How do we ensure successful process optimization?"

Jim appreciated Janet 's inquiry. "Ensuring successful

process optimization involves fostering a culture of continuous improvement and innovation, where employees are empowered to identify and implement cost-saving initiatives. Leaders must provide training and resources for employees, establish performance metrics to track progress, and celebrate successes to sustain momentum and drive results."

He continued to elaborate on the importance of process optimization in driving cost efficiency.

"Next," Jim said, clicking to the next slide, "we have **Strategic Sourcing**."

"Strategic sourcing," he explained, "involves evaluating supplier relationships, negotiating contracts, and leveraging economies of scale to achieve cost savings and improve quality and reliability of supply. Leaders must conduct supplier assessments, benchmark pricing, and develop strategic partnerships to optimize procurement processes and reduce total cost of ownership."

Richard Shaw, the head of sales, nodded in agreement. "How do we ensure successful strategic sourcing?"

"Ensuring successful strategic sourcing," Jim replied, "involves conducting thorough supplier evaluations, considering factors such as quality, reliability, and financial stability. Leaders must also foster open communication and collaboration with suppliers, negotiate favorable terms and pricing, and monitor supplier performance to ensure alignment with organizational goals and objectives."

He continued to discuss the importance of strategic sourcing in driving cost efficiency and competitiveness.

"As executives," Jim concluded, "it's essential for us to implement cost efficiency strategies to optimize our cost structure and drive sustainable growth for Cartwright Industries. By embracing process optimization and strategic sourcing, and fostering a culture of cost consciousness and innovation, we can maximize value for our stakeholders and strengthen our competitive position in the marketplace."

After Jim's presentation concluded, the room buzzed with focused energy as the team members exchanged ideas and insights on implementing cost efficiency strategies. They now had a clearer understanding of the importance of optimizing costs and their role in driving operational excellence for Cartwright Industries.

As the meeting adjourned, Jim felt a sense of determination. With a solid commitment to cost efficiency strategies, he knew that his team was well-equipped to identify opportunities for cost optimization, improve profitability, and drive sustainable growth for Cartwright Industries.

Case Studies in Operational Excellence

As the discussion on operational efficiency neared its conclusion, Jim Cartwright directed his senior management team's attention towards real-world case studies showcasing operational excellence in action. He knew that examining successful examples from various industries would provide valuable insights and inspiration for driving continuous improvement at Cartwright Industries.

"Good morning, everyone," Jim began, his voice filled with anticipation and eagerness. "Now, let's explore case studies in operational excellence and draw insights from successful examples that can guide us on our journey towards achieving operational excellence."

He clicked the remote, and the slide titled **Case Studies in**

Operational Excellence: Learning from the Best illuminated the screen.

"Let's start by understanding why case studies in operational excellence are crucial," Jim continued. "How can examining successful examples from other organizations help us identify best practices and apply them to our own operations?"

Paul Bennett, the COO, spoke up. "Studying case studies in operational excellence allows us to learn from the successes and failures of others, gain new perspectives, and identify innovative approaches to improving our processes. By analyzing real-world examples, we can glean valuable insights and best practices that we can adapt and apply to our own organization to drive continuous improvement and achieve operational excellence."

Jim nodded in agreement. "Exactly. Now, let's explore some case studies in operational excellence."

He clicked to the next slide, which displayed **Case Studies: Lessons Learned**.

"The first case study," Jim explained, "is **Toyota Production System (TPS)**."

"Toyota Production System," he continued, "is renowned for its focus on continuous improvement, waste reduction, and respect for people. By implementing principles such as just-in-time production, kanban, and jidoka (automation with a human touch), Toyota has achieved remarkable levels of efficiency, quality, and flexibility in its manufacturing operations."

Janet Ross, the HR Director, raised a question. "How can we apply the principles of TPS to our own operations?"

Jim appreciated Janet 's inquiry. "Applying the principles of TPS involves fostering a culture of continuous improvement and employee empowerment, where frontline employees are encouraged to identify and solve problems in real-time. Leaders must also focus on waste reduction, standardized work, and quality improvement to optimize processes and enhance overall performance."

He continued to elaborate on the lessons learned from Toyota's success in operational excellence.

"Next," Jim said, clicking to the next slide, "we have **Amazon's Fulfillment Centers**."

"Amazon's fulfillment centers," he explained, "are prime examples of operational excellence in the logistics and e-commerce industry. By leveraging advanced technology, automation, and data analytics, Amazon has optimized its fulfillment processes to deliver fast, reliable, and cost-effective service to customers worldwide."

Richard Shaw, the head of sales, nodded in agreement. "How can we leverage technology and automation like Amazon?"

"Leveraging technology and automation," Jim replied, "involves investing in advanced systems and tools to streamline processes, improve efficiency, and enhance customer experience. Leaders must also focus on data-driven decision-making, continuous innovation, and scalability to adapt to changing market dynamics and customer demands."

He continued to discuss the lessons learned from Amazon's success in operational excellence.

"As executives," Jim concluded, "it's essential for us to study case studies in operational excellence and draw insights from successful examples to inform our own improvement initiatives. By learning from the best, we can identify opportunities for innovation, optimize our processes, and achieve operational excellence for Cartwright Industries."

After Jim's presentation concluded, the room buzzed with excitement as the team members discussed the insights gained from the case studies. They now had a clearer understanding of the principles and practices of operational excellence and their relevance to Cartwright Industries.

As the meeting adjourned, Jim felt a sense of inspiration. With a solid foundation of knowledge and real-world examples to draw from, he knew that his team was well-prepared to drive continuous improvement and achieve operational excellence for Cartwright Industries.

11

Chapter 11: Leadership Communication

Effective Communication Skills

As the senior management team of Cartwright Industries gathered for their monthly leadership development session, Jim Cartwright, the CEO, set the stage for a crucial discussion on leadership communication. He understood that effective communication was the cornerstone of strong leadership and essential for driving organizational success.

"Good morning, everyone," Jim began, his voice commanding attention as he addressed the room. "Today, we embark on a journey to explore the importance of leadership communication and how it shapes our organization's culture and performance."

He clicked the remote, and the slide titled **Effective Communication Skills: Building Connection** illuminated the screen.

"Let's start by understanding why effective communication skills are crucial," Jim continued. "How can mastering communication techniques help us inspire, motivate, and engage our teams?"

Paul Bennett, the COO, spoke up. "Effective communication skills enable leaders to articulate their vision, build trust, and foster collaboration among team members. By listening actively, providing clear direction, and offering constructive feedback, leaders can create a positive work environment where employees feel valued and empowered to contribute their best."

Jim nodded in agreement. "Exactly. Now, let's explore the key components of effective communication skills."

He clicked to the next slide, which displayed **Key Components of Effective Communication Skills**.

"The first component," Jim explained, "is **Active Listening**. This involves fully concentrating on what others are saying, understanding their perspective, and responding thoughtfully. Leaders must practice empathy, ask clarifying questions, and avoid interrupting to demonstrate respect and foster open dialogue."

Janet Ross, the HR Director, raised a question. "How can we improve our active listening skills?"

Jim appreciated Janet's inquiry. "Improving active listening skills involves practicing mindfulness and being fully present in conversations. Leaders must also show genuine interest in others' viewpoints, validate their feelings, and summarize key points to ensure mutual understanding."

He continued to elaborate on the importance of active listening in effective communication.

"Next," Jim said, clicking to the next slide, "we have **Clarity**

and Conciseness."

"Clarity and conciseness," he explained, "involve delivering messages in a clear, straightforward manner that is easy for others to understand. Leaders must avoid jargon, use simple language, and organize their thoughts logically to convey their message effectively."

Richard Shaw, the head of sales, nodded in agreement. "How can we ensure that our messages are clear and concise?"

"Ensuring clear and concise communication," Jim replied, "involves preparing beforehand, organizing thoughts coherently, and focusing on the key points. Leaders must also anticipate questions or concerns and address them proactively to prevent misunderstandings."

He continued to discuss the importance of clarity and conciseness in effective communication.

"As executives," Jim concluded, "it's essential for us to master effective communication skills to inspire trust, foster collaboration, and drive organizational success. By practicing active listening, clarity, and conciseness, and fostering a culture of open communication and transparency, we can build stronger connections with our teams and achieve our strategic objectives."

After Jim's presentation concluded, the room buzzed with excitement as the team members discussed the importance of effective communication skills. They now had a clearer understanding of the critical role communication plays in leadership and organizational success.

As the meeting adjourned, Jim felt a sense of satisfaction. With a solid commitment to mastering communication techniques, he knew that his team was well-equipped to lead Cartwright Industries towards a brighter future.

Public Speaking and Presentations

With the foundation of effective communication skills laid out, Jim Cartwright shifted the focus of the leadership development session towards the importance of mastering public speaking and presentations. He recognized that the ability to convey messages confidently and persuasively in front of an audience was a vital skill for any leader.

"Good morning, everyone," Jim began, his voice projecting assurance and encouragement. "Now, let's delve into the realm of public speaking and presentations and how mastering these skills can enhance our leadership impact."

He clicked the remote, and the slide titled **Public Speaking and Presentations: Engaging Your Audience** illuminated the screen.

"Let's start by understanding why public speaking and presentation skills are crucial," Jim continued. "How can effectively delivering speeches and presentations help us influence and inspire others?"

Paul Bennett, the COO, spoke up. "Public speaking and presentations provide leaders with a platform to share their vision, inspire action, and build credibility with stakeholders. By delivering compelling messages, using engaging visuals, and connecting emotionally with the audience, leaders can captivate attention and drive desired outcomes."

Jim nodded in agreement. "Exactly. Now, let's explore the key components of mastering public speaking and presentations."

He clicked to the next slide, which displayed **Key Components of Public Speaking and Presentations**.

"The first component," Jim explained, "is **Confidence and**

Presence. This involves projecting confidence through body language, voice tone, and eye contact to establish credibility and authority. Leaders must practice relaxation techniques, visualize success, and adopt a positive mindset to exude confidence and presence."

Janet Ross, the HR Director, raised a question. "How can we overcome nervousness and anxiety when speaking in public?"

Jim appreciated Janet 's inquiry. "Overcoming nervousness and anxiety involves preparation, practice, and reframing negative thoughts. Leaders must also focus on the message and the audience, rather than on themselves, and embrace imperfection as part of the learning process."

He continued to elaborate on the importance of confidence and presence in public speaking.

"Next," Jim said, clicking to the next slide, "we have **Structure and Organization**."

"Structure and organization," he explained, "involve organizing thoughts logically and delivering messages in a clear, coherent manner. Leaders must create a compelling narrative, use storytelling techniques, and provide context and relevance to engage the audience and convey key points effectively."

Richard Shaw, the head of sales, nodded in agreement. "How can we ensure that our presentations are well-structured?"

"Ensuring well-structured presentations," Jim replied, "involves outlining key points, creating a clear introduction, body, and conclusion, and using visual aids strategically to enhance understanding and retention. Leaders must also practice time management and prioritize information to keep the audience engaged and focused."

He continued to discuss the importance of structure and organization in effective presentations.

"As executives," Jim concluded, "it's essential for us to master public speaking and presentation skills to inspire and influence others effectively. By projecting confidence and presence, and delivering well-structured presentations, we can engage our audience, convey our message persuasively, and achieve our desired outcomes."

After Jim's presentation concluded, the room buzzed with enthusiasm as the team members discussed strategies for improving their public speaking and presentation skills. They now had a clearer understanding of the key components of effective communication in a public setting.

As the meeting adjourned, Jim felt a sense of optimism. With a solid commitment to mastering public speaking and presentations, he knew that his team was well-prepared to elevate their leadership communication and make a lasting impact at Cartwright Industries.

Communicating with Different Stakeholders

As the discussion on communication skills continued, Jim Cartwright transitioned the focus towards the importance of tailoring communication to different stakeholders. He understood that effective leaders must adapt their messaging and approach to resonate with various audiences.

"Good morning, everyone," Jim began, his voice projecting a sense of adaptability and versatility. "Now, let's explore the art of communicating with different stakeholders and how it contributes to our effectiveness as leaders."

He clicked the remote, and the slide titled **Communicating with Different Stakeholders: Building Relationships** illuminated the screen.

"Let's start by understanding why communicating with different stakeholders is crucial," Jim continued. "How can adapting our communication style help us build stronger relationships and achieve our organizational goals?"

Paul Bennett, the COO, spoke up. "Communicating with different stakeholders allows us to tailor our messages to their specific needs, interests, and preferences. By understanding their perspectives, addressing their concerns, and building rapport, leaders can establish trust and credibility, which are essential for driving collaboration and achieving shared objectives."

Jim nodded in agreement. "Exactly. Now, let's explore the key components of communicating with different stakeholders."

He clicked to the next slide, which displayed **Key Components of Communicating with Different Stakeholders**.

"The first component," Jim explained, "is **Audience Analysis**. This involves understanding the backgrounds, interests, and communication preferences of different stakeholders. Leaders must conduct research, ask questions, and listen actively to gain insights into their perspectives and tailor their messages accordingly."

Janet Ross, the HR Director, raised a question. "How can we adapt our communication style to different stakeholders?"

Jim appreciated Janet 's inquiry. "Adapting our communication style involves using appropriate language, tone, and messaging to resonate with the audience. Leaders must be empathetic, flexible, and authentic in their communication, and adjust their approach based on the needs and expectations of different stakeholders."

He continued to elaborate on the importance of audience

analysis in effective communication.

"Next," Jim said, clicking to the next slide, "we have **Customization and Personalization**."

"Customization and personalization," he explained, "involve tailoring messages to address the specific interests and concerns of different stakeholders. Leaders must use storytelling, examples, and analogies to make their messages relatable and meaningful to the audience, and highlight the benefits or implications of their ideas or proposals."

Richard Shaw, the head of sales, nodded in agreement. "How can we ensure that our messages resonate with different stakeholders?"

"Ensuring that our messages resonate," Jim replied, "involves seeking feedback, being open to dialogue, and adjusting our approach based on the response. Leaders must also demonstrate empathy and understanding, acknowledge diverse perspectives, and seek common ground to foster collaboration and alignment."

He continued to discuss the importance of customization and personalization in effective communication.

"As executives," Jim concluded, "it's essential for us to master the art of communicating with different stakeholders to build stronger relationships and achieve our organizational goals. By conducting audience analysis, and customizing and personalizing our messages, we can establish trust, foster collaboration, and drive collective success."

After Jim's presentation concluded, the room buzzed with excitement as the team members discussed strategies for adapting their communication to different stakeholders. They now had a clearer understanding of the importance of tailoring messages to resonate with diverse audiences.

As the meeting adjourned, Jim felt a sense of satisfaction. With a solid commitment to understanding and connecting with different stakeholders, he knew that his team was well-equipped to navigate complex communication challenges and drive success at Cartwright Industries.

Feedback and Active Listening

As the discussion on communication skills progressed, Jim Cartwright directed the focus towards the importance of feedback and active listening in effective communication. He understood that creating a culture of open feedback and listening attentively were essential for fostering trust and collaboration within the organization.

"Good morning, everyone," Jim began, his voice resonating with attentiveness and openness. "Now, let's delve into the vital aspects of feedback and active listening in our communication practices and how they contribute to our leadership effectiveness."

He clicked the remote, and the slide titled **Feedback and Active Listening: Strengthening Connections** illuminated the screen.

"Let's start by understanding why feedback and active listening are crucial," Jim continued. "How can cultivating these skills help us build stronger relationships and enhance our communication effectiveness?"

Paul Bennett, the COO, spoke up. "Feedback and active listening create an environment of trust, transparency, and collaboration. By actively seeking and providing feedback, and listening attentively to others' perspectives, leaders can demonstrate empathy, build rapport, and foster a culture of continuous improvement and learning within the organization."

Jim nodded in agreement. "Exactly. Now, let's explore the key components of feedback and active listening."

He clicked to the next slide, which displayed **Key Components of Feedback and Active Listening**.

"The first component," Jim explained, "is **Seeking Feedback**. This involves actively soliciting input, suggestions, and opinions from others to gain insights into their experiences and perspectives. Leaders must create opportunities for feedback, ask open-ended questions, and demonstrate a willingness to listen and learn from others."

Janet Ross, the HR Director, raised a question. "How can we encourage a culture of open feedback?"

Jim appreciated Janet 's inquiry. "Encouraging a culture of open feedback involves setting the example as leaders, providing constructive feedback, and creating a safe and supportive environment where employees feel empowered to share their thoughts and ideas. Leaders must also be receptive to feedback, acknowledge contributions, and take action on suggestions to demonstrate their commitment to continuous improvement."

He continued to elaborate on the importance of seeking feedback in effective communication.

"Next," Jim said, clicking to the next slide, "we have **Active Listening**."

"Active listening," he explained, "involves fully concentrating on what others are saying, understanding their perspective, and responding thoughtfully. Leaders must listen with an open mind, maintain eye contact, and refrain from interrupting to show respect and empathy towards the speaker."

Richard Shaw, the head of sales, nodded in agreement. "How can we improve our active listening skills?"

"Improving active listening skills," Jim replied, "involves practicing mindfulness and being fully present in conversations. Leaders must also ask clarifying questions, paraphrase what they've heard, and provide feedback to ensure mutual understanding and reinforce trust and rapport."

He continued to discuss the importance of active listening in effective communication.

"As executives," Jim concluded, "it's essential for us to cultivate feedback and active listening skills to build stronger connections and enhance our communication effectiveness. By seeking feedback, and actively listening to others' perspectives, we can foster trust, collaboration, and a culture of continuous improvement within our organization."

After Jim's presentation concluded, the room buzzed with enthusiasm as the team members discussed strategies for incorporating feedback and active listening into their communication practices. They now had a clearer understanding of the importance of creating an environment of openness and receptivity.

As the meeting adjourned, Jim felt a sense of optimism. With a solid commitment to feedback and active listening, he knew that his team was well-equipped to foster trust and collaboration and drive success at Cartwright Industries.

Managing Internal and External Communications

As the conversation on communication skills evolved, Jim Cartwright turned the discussion towards the critical aspect of managing both internal and external communications within the organization. He recognized that effective communication with both audiences was essential for maintaining transparency, alignment, and trust.

"Good morning, everyone," Jim began, his voice projecting a sense of purpose and clarity. "Now, let's explore the importance of managing both internal and external communications and how they contribute to our organizational success."

He clicked the remote, and the slide titled **Managing Internal and External Communications: Building Trust** illuminated the screen.

"Let's start by understanding why managing internal and external communications is crucial," Jim continued. "How can effectively communicating with both audiences help us achieve our strategic objectives and strengthen our relationships?"

Paul Bennett, the COO, spoke up. "Managing internal communications ensures that employees are informed, engaged, and aligned with our organizational goals and priorities. By providing clear, timely updates and fostering open dialogue, we can boost morale, productivity, and retention. Similarly, managing external communications allows us to build and maintain positive relationships with stakeholders such as customers, investors, and the media, enhancing our reputation and credibility in the marketplace."

Jim nodded in agreement. "Exactly. Now, let's explore the key components of managing internal and external communications."

He clicked to the next slide, which displayed **Key Components of Managing Internal and External Communications**.

"The first component," Jim explained, "is **Transparency**

and Consistency. This involves being open and honest in our communications, sharing information proactively, and maintaining consistency in our messaging across all channels. Leaders must ensure that employees and external stakeholders receive accurate, timely, and relevant information to foster trust and confidence in our organization."

Janet Ross, the HR Director, raised a question. "How can we ensure transparency in our communications?"

Jim appreciated Janet 's inquiry. "Ensuring transparency," he replied, "involves being authentic, admitting mistakes, and addressing concerns openly. Leaders must also provide context and rationale for decisions, actively listen to feedback, and communicate with empathy and respect to build trust and credibility with both internal and external audiences."

He continued to elaborate on the importance of transparency and consistency in communication.

"Next," Jim said, clicking to the next slide, "we have **Tailoring Messages to Audience**."

"Tailoring messages to audience," he explained, "involves understanding the needs, interests, and preferences of different stakeholders and customizing our communications accordingly. Leaders must use language and tone appropriate for the audience, highlight relevant benefits or implications, and address specific concerns or questions to ensure clarity and relevance."

Richard Shaw, the head of sales, nodded in agreement. "How can we maintain consistency in our external communications?"

"Maintaining consistency," Jim replied, "involves developing a clear brand voice and messaging framework, and ensuring alignment across all communication channels, including press releases, social media, and marketing materials. Leaders must also train employees to be brand ambassadors and provide guidelines and resources to support consistent messaging and brand representation."

He continued to discuss the importance of tailoring messages to audience in effective communication.

"As executives," Jim concluded, "it's essential for us to manage both internal and external communications effectively to build trust, credibility, and alignment within our organization and with external stakeholders. By prioritizing transparency and consistency, and tailoring messages to audience, we can strengthen our relationships, enhance our reputation, and achieve our strategic objectives."

After Jim's presentation concluded, the room buzzed with enthusiasm as the team members discussed strategies for improving both internal and external communications. They now had a clearer understanding of the importance of managing communication effectively to drive organizational success.

As the meeting adjourned, Jim felt a sense of satisfaction. With a solid commitment to transparency, consistency, and audience tailoring, he knew that his team was well-prepared to navigate the complexities of communication and achieve their goals at Cartwright Industries.

Communication Tools and Technologies

As the conversation on communication skills reached its final subpoint, Jim Cartwright directed the team's focus to the importance of leveraging modern communication tools and technologies. He recognized that utilizing the right tools could enhance efficiency, clarity, and reach, making communication more effective both internally and externally.

"Good morning, everyone," Jim began, his voice infused with enthusiasm and forward-thinking. "For our last discussion today, let's explore the various communication tools and technologies available to us and how they can improve our communication practices."

He clicked the remote, and the slide titled **Communication Tools and Technologies: Enhancing Connectivity** illuminated the screen.

"Let's start by understanding why leveraging communication tools and technologies is crucial," Jim continued. "How can utilizing these tools help us communicate more effectively and efficiently?"

Paul Bennett, the COO, spoke up. "Using modern communication tools allows us to streamline our communication processes, improve real-time collaboration, and reach a broader audience. By leveraging technologies such as video conferencing, instant messaging, and project management software, we can enhance productivity, reduce misunderstandings, and foster a more connected and responsive organizational culture."

Jim nodded in agreement. "Exactly. Now, let's explore the key components of effectively using communication tools and technologies."

He clicked to the next slide, which displayed **Key Components of Communication Tools and Technologies**.

"The first component," Jim explained, "is **Selection of Appropriate Tools**. This involves identifying and selecting the right communication tools based on the specific needs and preferences of our teams and stakeholders. Leaders must evaluate the features, benefits, and potential challenges of different tools to ensure they align with our communication goals and organizational culture."

Janet Ross, the HR Director, raised a question. "How can we determine which tools are best suited for our needs?"

Jim appreciated Janet 's inquiry. "Determining the best-suited tools involves assessing the communication needs of various departments, gathering feedback from employees, and conducting pilot tests to evaluate usability and effectiveness. Leaders must also consider factors such as ease of integration, security, and scalability to ensure the selected tools support our long-term communication strategies."

He continued to elaborate on the importance of selecting appropriate tools.

"Next," Jim said, clicking to the next slide, "we have **Training and Adoption**."

"Training and adoption," he explained, "involves providing comprehensive training and support to ensure employees can effectively use the selected communication tools. Leaders must offer hands-on workshops, create user guides, and provide ongoing support to address any issues and encourage adoption."

Richard Shaw, the head of sales, nodded in agreement. "How can we ensure that employees adopt and effectively use these tools?"

"Ensuring adoption and effective use," Jim replied, "involves creating a positive attitude towards new tools, demonstrating their benefits, and integrating them into daily workflows. Leaders must also lead by example, use the tools consistently, and recognize and reward employees who effectively utilize them to reinforce positive behavior."

He continued to discuss the importance of training and

adoption in effective communication.

"As executives," Jim concluded, "it's essential for us to leverage communication tools and technologies to enhance our connectivity and efficiency. By selecting the appropriate tools and ensuring their effective adoption, we can improve real-time collaboration, reduce misunderstandings, and foster a more connected and responsive organizational culture."

After Jim's presentation concluded, the room buzzed with excitement as the team members discussed strategies for integrating communication tools and technologies into their workflows. They now had a clearer understanding of the importance of leveraging modern tools to drive effective communication.

As the meeting adjourned, Jim felt a sense of optimism. With a solid commitment to selecting and adopting the right communication tools, he knew that his team was well-prepared to enhance their connectivity, efficiency, and overall communication effectiveness at Cartwright Industries.

12

Chapter 12: Corporate Social Responsibility

Defining CSR

J im Cartwright stood at the head of the conference room, his expression serious yet energized. Today's session would delve into a topic that had become increasingly crucial in the modern business landscape—Corporate Social Responsibility (CSR).

"Good morning, everyone," Jim began, his voice resonating with purpose. "Today, we're going to explore Corporate Social Responsibility, or CSR, and its role in our business strategy. We'll start with the fundamentals: defining what CSR truly means."

He clicked the remote, and the slide titled **Defining CSR: Building a Responsible Business** illuminated the screen.

"To begin, let's consider why understanding and defining CSR is important," Jim continued. "Why is it crucial for us as leaders to integrate CSR into our organizational framework?"

Paul Bennett, the COO, spoke up. "CSR is about more than just ethical practices or philanthropy; it's about embedding responsibility into the core of our business operations. It's essential because it aligns our business objectives with the expectations of society, enhances our reputation, and ultimately contributes to sustainable success."

Jim nodded in agreement. "Exactly. Now, let's break down what CSR entails."

He clicked to the next slide, which displayed **Key Components of CSR.**

"The first component," Jim explained, "is **Ethical Practices**. This involves ensuring that our business operations are conducted with integrity, fairness, and respect for all stakeholders, including employees, customers, suppliers, and the community."

Janet Ross, the HR Director, raised a question. "How can we ensure that our ethical practices are aligned with CSR principles?"

Jim appreciated Janet 's inquiry. "Ensuring alignment with CSR principles involves establishing a clear code of conduct, providing ethics training, and promoting a culture of transparency and accountability. Leaders must also actively monitor compliance and address any ethical concerns promptly and effectively."

He continued to elaborate on the importance of ethical practices.

"Next," Jim said, clicking to the next slide, "we have **Environmental Responsibility**."

"Environmental responsibility," he explained, "involves implementing sustainable practices that minimize our ecological footprint and contribute positively to environmental conservation. Leaders must focus on reducing waste, conserving resources, and promoting green initiatives within the organization."

Richard Shaw, the head of sales, nodded in agreement. "How can we incorporate environmental responsibility into our business strategy?"

"Incorporating environmental responsibility," Jim replied, "involves setting measurable sustainability goals, investing in eco-friendly technologies, and engaging employees in green practices. Leaders must also collaborate with partners and stakeholders to drive broader environmental impact."

He continued to discuss the importance of environmental responsibility.

"As executives," Jim concluded, "it's essential for us to define and embrace CSR to build a responsible and sustainable business. By focusing on ethical practices and environmental responsibility, we can enhance our reputation, meet societal expectations, and contribute to long-term success."

After Jim's presentation concluded, the room buzzed with enthusiasm as the team members discussed strategies for defining and integrating CSR into their business operations. They now had a clearer understanding of the importance of embedding responsibility into the core of their business practices.

As the meeting adjourned, Jim felt a sense of determination. With a solid commitment to defining and embracing CSR, he knew that his team was well-prepared to build a responsible and sustainable business at Cartwright Industries.

Creating a CSR Strategy

As the initial discussion on defining Corporate Social Responsibility (CSR) wrapped up, Jim Cartwright could see a renewed sense of purpose in the room. Now it was time to move from definition to action—creating a robust CSR strategy for Cartwright Industries.

"Good morning again, everyone," Jim began, his tone steady and focused. "Now that we've defined what CSR means for us, the next step is to create a comprehensive CSR strategy that aligns with our business objectives and societal expectations."

He clicked the remote, and the slide titled **Creating a CSR Strategy: Turning Vision into Action** appeared on the screen.

"To start, let's consider why developing a CSR strategy is crucial," Jim continued. "How can a well-crafted CSR strategy benefit our organization and our stakeholders?"

Paul Bennett, the COO, was quick to respond. "A clear CSR strategy provides direction and purpose, ensuring that our efforts are coordinated and impactful. It helps us prioritize initiatives, allocate resources effectively, and measure our progress. Moreover, it strengthens our reputation, attracts talent, and builds trust with our stakeholders."

Jim nodded appreciatively. "Exactly. Now, let's break down the key steps in creating a successful CSR strategy."

He clicked to the next slide, which displayed **Key Steps in Creating a CSR Strategy**.

"The first step," Jim explained, "is **Identifying Key Areas of Impact**. This involves understanding the social, environmental, and economic issues that are most relevant to our business and stakeholders. Leaders must conduct thorough assessments to identify areas where our actions can make the most significant positive impact."

Janet Ross, the HR Director, raised a question. "How can we effectively identify these key areas of impact?"

Jim appreciated Janet's inquiry. "Effectively identifying key areas of impact involves engaging with stakeholders through surveys, focus groups, and consultations. We must also conduct internal and external audits to assess our current impact and opportunities for improvement. Benchmarking against industry standards and best practices can also provide valuable insights."

He continued to elaborate on the importance of identifying key areas of impact.

"Next," Jim said, clicking to the next slide, "we have **Setting Clear Goals and Objectives**."

"Setting clear goals and objectives," he explained, "involves defining specific, measurable, achievable, relevant, and time-bound (SMART) goals for our CSR initiatives. Leaders must ensure that these goals align with our overall business strategy and reflect our commitment to making a positive impact."

Richard Shaw, the head of sales, nodded in agreement. "How can we ensure that our CSR goals are both ambitious and realistic?"

"Ensuring that our CSR goals are ambitious yet realistic," Jim replied, "involves balancing aspiration with practicality. Leaders must set challenging goals that inspire progress but are grounded in a realistic assessment of our capabilities and resources. Regularly reviewing and adjusting goals based on feedback and results is also crucial."

He continued to discuss the importance of setting clear goals and objectives.

"As executives," Jim concluded, "it's essential for us to create a well-defined CSR strategy that guides our efforts and maximizes our positive impact. By identifying key areas of impact and setting clear goals, we can turn our vision into action and drive meaningful change."

After Jim's presentation concluded, the room buzzed with energy as the team members discussed strategies for developing and implementing a comprehensive CSR strategy. They now had a clearer understanding of the importance of creating a well-defined plan to guide their CSR efforts.

As the meeting adjourned, Jim felt a sense of optimism. With a solid commitment to creating and executing a robust CSR strategy, he knew that his team was well-prepared to lead Cartwright Industries towards a more responsible and sustainable future.

Integrating CSR with Business Goals

After discussing the initial steps of defining CSR and creating a strategy, Jim Cartwright was eager to address the next critical phase: integrating CSR initiatives with the company's core business goals. This integration was essential for ensuring that CSR was not just an add-on but a fundamental part of Cartwright Industries' operational ethos.

"Good morning once more," Jim began, his voice firm and compelling. "Now that we've defined CSR and laid out our strategy, it's time to explore how we can seamlessly integrate CSR into our business goals to ensure it becomes an intrinsic part of everything we do."

He clicked the remote, and the slide titled **Integrating CSR with Business Goals: Aligning Purpose and Profit** appeared on the screen.

"To start, let's consider why integrating CSR with our business goals is crucial," Jim continued. "How does this integration benefit our organization and enhance our impact?"

Paul Bennett, the COO, was quick to respond. "Integrating CSR with business goals ensures that our CSR initiatives are aligned with our core mission and values. This alignment not only reinforces our commitment to ethical and sustainable practices but also enhances our competitiveness, drives innovation, and creates long-term value for our stakeholders."

Jim nodded appreciatively. "Exactly. Now, let's delve into the key strategies for successfully integrating CSR with our business goals."

He clicked to the next slide, which displayed **Key Strategies for Integrating CSR with Business Goals**.

"The first strategy," Jim explained, "is **Aligning CSR Initiatives with Business Strategy**. This involves ensuring that our CSR goals and initiatives are directly linked to our overall business strategy and objectives. Leaders must identify synergies between CSR activities and business operations to create a cohesive approach."

Janet Ross, the HR Director, raised a question. "How can we ensure that our CSR initiatives are effectively aligned with our business strategy?"

Jim appreciated Janet's inquiry. "Ensuring effective alignment involves conducting a thorough review of our business strategy and identifying areas where CSR can support and enhance our goals. Leaders must also engage with cross-functional teams to integrate CSR considerations into decision-making processes and strategic planning."

He continued to elaborate on the importance of aligning

CSR initiatives with the business strategy.

"Next," Jim said, clicking to the next slide, "we have **Embedding CSR into Corporate Culture**."

"Embedding CSR into corporate culture," he explained, "involves fostering a culture where social and environmental responsibility is ingrained in our values, behaviors, and practices. Leaders must lead by example, promote awareness, and encourage employee engagement in CSR activities."

Richard Shaw, the head of sales, nodded in agreement. "How can we effectively embed CSR into our corporate culture?"

"Effectively embedding CSR into our corporate culture," Jim replied, "involves developing and communicating a clear CSR vision, providing training and resources, and recognizing and rewarding employees who contribute to CSR initiatives. Leaders must also create opportunities for employees to participate in CSR activities and integrate CSR metrics into performance evaluations."

He continued to discuss the importance of embedding CSR into corporate culture.

"As executives," Jim concluded, "it's essential for us to integrate CSR with our business goals to ensure that our efforts are cohesive, impactful, and sustainable. By aligning CSR initiatives with our business strategy and embedding CSR into our corporate culture, we can drive meaningful change and create long-term value for our organization and stakeholders."

After Jim's presentation concluded, the room buzzed with excitement as the team members discussed strategies for integrating CSR with their business goals. They now had a clearer understanding of the importance of aligning their efforts to create a cohesive and impactful approach to CSR.

As the meeting adjourned, Jim felt a sense of optimism. With a solid commitment to integrating CSR with their business goals, he knew that his team was well-prepared to lead Cartwright Industries towards a future where purpose and profit were harmoniously aligned.

Measuring CSR Impact

Having explored the strategies for integrating CSR into Cartwright Industries' business goals, Jim Cartwright was ready to address a crucial aspect of any CSR initiative— measuring its impact. This step was vital to ensure that their efforts were making a tangible difference and to guide future initiatives.

"Good afternoon, everyone," Jim began, his voice filled with determination. "Now that we've discussed integrating CSR with our business goals, the next step is to focus on how we measure the impact of our CSR activities. Without proper measurement, we can't truly understand the effectiveness of our initiatives or make informed decisions about where to direct our efforts."

He clicked the remote, and the slide titled **Measuring CSR Impact: Evaluating Effectiveness and Guiding Future Efforts** appeared on the screen.

"To start, let's consider why measuring CSR impact is essential," Jim continued. "How does measurement help us enhance our CSR initiatives and ensure accountability?"

Paul Bennett, the COO, spoke up. "Measuring CSR impact allows us to assess the effectiveness of our initiatives, identify areas for improvement, and demonstrate accountability to our stakeholders. It also provides valuable insights that can guide our future efforts and ensure that our resources are being used efficiently."

Jim nodded in agreement. "Precisely. Now, let's delve into the key methods for measuring the impact of our CSR activities."

He clicked to the next slide, which displayed **Key Methods for Measuring CSR Impact**.

"The first method," Jim explained, "is **Defining Key Performance Indicators (KPIs)**. This involves identifying specific, measurable indicators that can track the progress and impact of our CSR initiatives. These KPIs should align with our overall business and CSR goals and be relevant to the specific activities we are undertaking."

Janet Ross, the HR Director, raised a question. "How can we ensure that our KPIs are comprehensive and meaningful?"

Jim appreciated Janet's inquiry. "Ensuring comprehensive and meaningful KPIs involves engaging with stakeholders to understand their expectations and priorities, reviewing industry standards and best practices, and regularly revisiting and refining our KPIs based on feedback and results. It's important to strike a balance between quantitative and qualitative measures to capture the full scope of our impact."

He continued to elaborate on the importance of defining KPIs.

"Next," Jim said, clicking to the next slide, "we have **Collecting and Analyzing Data**."

"Collecting and analyzing data," he explained, "involves gathering relevant information on our CSR activities and their outcomes. Leaders must establish robust data collection processes, utilize appropriate tools and technologies, and ensure the accuracy and reliability of the data."

Richard Shaw, the head of sales, nodded in agreement. "How can we ensure the accuracy and reliability of the data we collect?"

"Ensuring accuracy and reliability," Jim replied, "involves standardizing data collection methods, providing training and support to those responsible for data collection, and implementing regular audits and reviews. Utilizing technology such as data analytics software can also enhance our ability to analyze and interpret the data effectively."

He continued to discuss the importance of collecting and analyzing data.

"As executives," Jim concluded, "it's essential for us to measure the impact of our CSR initiatives to ensure their effectiveness and guide our future efforts. By defining clear KPIs and establishing robust data collection and analysis processes, we can gain valuable insights, demonstrate accountability, and continually improve our CSR strategy."

After Jim's presentation concluded, the room was filled with a sense of determination as the team members discussed strategies for measuring the impact of their CSR activities. They now had a clearer understanding of the importance of robust measurement practices to enhance their CSR initiatives.

As the meeting adjourned, Jim felt a sense of confidence. With a solid commitment to measuring and analyzing their CSR impact, he knew that his team was well-prepared to lead Cartwright Industries towards a future where their CSR efforts were not only meaningful but also demonstrably effective.

Engaging with Communities

Having covered the essentials of measuring CSR impact, Jim Cartwright was eager to delve into a critical aspect of Corporate Social Responsibility—engaging with the communities they served. This engagement was not just about giving back, but about fostering strong, mutually beneficial relationships.

"Good afternoon once again, everyone," Jim began, his voice carrying a warm yet determined tone. "Today, we'll discuss a vital component of our CSR strategy: engaging with communities. Our relationship with the communities we operate in is essential for creating a positive impact and ensuring our CSR efforts are truly meaningful."

He clicked the remote, and the slide titled **Engaging with Communities: Building Lasting Relationships** appeared on the screen.

"To start, let's consider why engaging with communities is crucial," Jim continued. "What benefits do we gain from strong community relationships?"

Paul Bennett, the COO, responded thoughtfully. "Engaging with communities helps us understand their needs and expectations, fosters goodwill, and enhances our reputation. It also creates opportunities for collaboration and innovation, allowing us to address local issues effectively and contribute to the community's well-being."

Jim nodded in agreement. "Exactly. Now, let's explore the key strategies for effectively engaging with communities."

He clicked to the next slide, which displayed **Key Strategies for Community Engagement**.

"The first strategy," Jim explained, "is **Understanding Community Needs**. This involves conducting thorough

211

assessments to identify the specific needs and priorities of the communities we operate in. Leaders must engage with community members through surveys, focus groups, and town hall meetings to gather valuable insights."

Janet Ross, the HR Director, raised a question. "How can we ensure that we are accurately understanding and addressing community needs?"

Jim appreciated Janet's inquiry. "Ensuring accurate understanding and addressing community needs involves continuous dialogue and feedback loops. We must build trust by being transparent and responsive, and by demonstrating our commitment to addressing their concerns. Regularly revisiting and updating our assessments based on new information is also crucial."

He continued to elaborate on the importance of understanding community needs.

"Next," Jim said, clicking to the next slide, "we have **Collaborative Initiatives**."

"Collaborative initiatives," he explained, "involve partnering with local organizations, schools, and non-profits to co-create programs that address community challenges. Leaders must seek out and foster these partnerships to leverage local knowledge and resources effectively."

Richard Shaw, the head of sales, nodded in agreement. "How can we establish and maintain effective partnerships with local organizations?"

"Establishing and maintaining effective partnerships," Jim replied, "involves identifying common goals, maintaining open communication, and ensuring mutual respect and benefit. Leaders must also be willing to invest time and resources into these relationships and be flexible and adaptive to changing circumstances and needs."

He continued to discuss the importance of collaborative initiatives.

"As executives," Jim concluded, "it's essential for us to engage with communities to build lasting relationships and create meaningful impact. By understanding community needs and fostering collaborative initiatives, we can ensure our CSR efforts are aligned with the expectations and well-being of those we serve."

After Jim's presentation concluded, the room buzzed with enthusiasm as the team members discussed strategies for engaging with their communities. They now had a clearer understanding of the importance of building strong, mutually beneficial relationships with local stakeholders.

As the meeting adjourned, Jim felt a sense of fulfillment. With a solid commitment to engaging with communities, he knew that his team was well-prepared to lead Cartwright Industries towards a future where their CSR efforts were deeply connected to and valued by the communities they aimed to support.

Reporting and Transparency

Having delved into the importance of engaging with communities, Jim Cartwright knew that the final piece of their CSR strategy was crucial—reporting and transparency. It was time to discuss how Cartwright Industries would communicate its CSR efforts and results, ensuring accountability and building trust.

"Good afternoon once more, everyone," Jim began, his tone firm yet inviting. "As we wrap up our discussion on Corporate

Social Responsibility, our final focus will be on reporting and transparency. It's essential that we not only carry out our CSR initiatives effectively but also communicate our progress openly and honestly."

He clicked the remote, and the slide titled **Reporting and Transparency: Building Trust and Accountability** appeared on the screen.

"To start, let's consider why reporting and transparency are vital," Jim continued. "How do they enhance our CSR efforts and impact?"

Paul Bennett, the COO, was quick to respond. "Reporting and transparency ensure that we are accountable for our actions and outcomes. They build trust with our stakeholders by showing that we are committed to ethical practices and willing to share our successes and areas for improvement. This openness also encourages continuous improvement and stakeholder engagement."

Jim nodded appreciatively. "Exactly. Now, let's explore the key components of effective CSR reporting and transparency."

He clicked to the next slide, which displayed **Key Components of Effective CSR Reporting and Transparency**.

"The first component," Jim explained, "is **Regular Reporting**. This involves establishing a schedule for reporting our CSR activities and outcomes. Leaders must ensure that these reports are timely, consistent, and accessible to all stakeholders."

Janet Ross, the HR Director, raised a question. "How can we ensure that our CSR reports are both comprehensive and accessible?"

Jim appreciated Janet 's inquiry. "Ensuring that our CSR reports are comprehensive and accessible involves using clear, straightforward language and visual aids to communicate complex information. Leaders must also make these reports available through multiple channels, such as our website, social media, and stakeholder meetings, to reach a broad audience."

He continued to elaborate on the importance of regular reporting.

"Next," Jim said, clicking to the next slide, "we have **Transparency in Communication**."

"Transparency in communication," he explained, "involves being open about our goals, methods, and challenges. Leaders must provide honest assessments of our progress and be willing to share both successes and setbacks. This transparency builds credibility and trust with our stakeholders."

Richard Shaw, the head of sales, nodded in agreement. "How can we balance transparency with protecting sensitive information?"

"Balancing transparency with protecting sensitive information," Jim replied, "involves clearly defining what information can be shared and what must remain confidential. Leaders must ensure that sensitive data is protected while still being as open as possible about our CSR efforts. Establishing clear guidelines and protocols for reporting can help manage this balance."

He continued to discuss the importance of transparency in communication.

"As executives," Jim concluded, "it's essential for us to report our CSR activities and outcomes transparently to build trust and accountability. By committing to regular reporting and transparent communication, we can demonstrate our dedication to ethical practices and continuous improvement."

After Jim's presentation concluded, the room buzzed with agreement as the team members discussed strategies for enhancing their CSR reporting and transparency. They now had a clearer understanding of the importance of open, honest communication in building trust and demonstrating accountability.

As the meeting adjourned, Jim felt a sense of confidence. With a solid commitment to reporting and transparency, he knew that his team was well-prepared to lead Cartwright Industries towards a future where their CSR efforts were not only impactful but also trusted and respected by all their stakeholders.

13

Chapter 13: Technology and Digital Transformation

The Role of Technology in Business

J im Cartwright stood at the head of the conference table, the hum of anticipation filling the room. Today's topic was a pivotal one—how technology could propel Cartwright Industries into the future. He knew that embracing digital transformation was no longer optional; it was essential for survival and growth in the modern business landscape.

"Good morning, everyone," Jim began, his voice resonating with excitement and urgency. "Today, we embark on a crucial discussion about the role of technology in our business. In this rapidly evolving world, our ability to leverage technology will determine our competitiveness and success."

He clicked the remote, and the slide titled **The Role of Technology in Business: Driving Innovation and Efficiency** appeared on the screen.

"To start, let's consider why technology is so critical for businesses today," Jim continued. "What advantages does it bring, and how can it transform our operations?"

Paul Bennett, the COO, leaned forward, ready to contribute. "Technology enhances our efficiency by automating routine tasks, reducing errors, and speeding up processes. It also drives innovation by providing tools for better data analysis, enabling us to make informed decisions and develop new products and services."

Jim nodded in agreement. "Exactly. Now, let's delve into the specific ways technology can impact our business."

He clicked to the next slide, which displayed **Key Benefits of Technology in Business**.

"The first benefit," Jim explained, "is **Improved Operational Efficiency**. Technology allows us to streamline our processes, reduce waste, and improve productivity. For instance, automation tools can handle repetitive tasks, freeing up our employees to focus on more strategic activities."

Janet Ross, the HR Director, raised a question. "How can we ensure that our employees are ready to adapt to new technologies and use them effectively?"

Jim appreciated Janet 's inquiry. "Ensuring that our employees are ready involves providing comprehensive training and support. Leaders must invest in ongoing education and create a culture that embraces change and continuous learning. Additionally, involving employees in the technology selection and implementation process can help them feel more engaged and comfortable with new tools."

He continued to elaborate on the importance of improving operational efficiency through technology.

"Next," Jim said, clicking to the next slide, "we have **En-**

hanced Data Analysis and Decision-Making."

"Enhanced data analysis and decision-making," he explained, "involves using advanced analytics tools to gather and interpret data. This capability allows us to identify trends, make predictions, and base our decisions on solid evidence rather than intuition alone."

Richard Shaw, the head of sales, nodded in agreement. "How can we effectively integrate data analytics into our decision-making processes?"

"Effectively integrating data analytics," Jim replied, "involves building a robust data infrastructure and ensuring that relevant data is accessible to decision-makers. Leaders must also promote a data-driven culture where decisions are based on insights rather than assumptions. Providing training on data analysis tools and techniques is also essential."

He continued to discuss the importance of enhanced data analysis and decision-making.

"As executives," Jim concluded, "it's essential for us to understand and harness the role of technology in our business. By improving operational efficiency and enhancing our decision-making capabilities, we can drive innovation, stay competitive, and achieve long-term success."

After Jim's presentation concluded, the room buzzed with enthusiasm as the team members discussed strategies for leveraging technology in their respective departments. They now had a clearer understanding of the critical role that technology would play in the future of Cartwright Industries.

As the meeting adjourned, Jim felt a renewed sense of optimism. With a solid commitment to embracing technology and digital transformation, he knew that his team was well-prepared to lead Cartwright Industries towards a future of innovation, efficiency, and success.

Digital Transformation Strategies

Jim Cartwright felt the weight of the moment as he prepared to dive into the next part of their journey—developing and implementing digital transformation strategies. His team had grasped the importance of technology in business, and now it was time to translate that understanding into actionable strategies.

"Good afternoon, everyone," Jim began, his voice steady and resolute. "Our discussion today focuses on the next critical step: digital transformation strategies. We know the importance of technology, but to truly harness its potential, we need a clear, strategic approach."

He clicked the remote, and the slide titled **Digital Transformation Strategies: Planning for Success** appeared on the screen.

"To start, let's discuss why having a digital transformation strategy is crucial," Jim continued. "Why can't we just adopt new technologies as they come along?"

Paul Bennett, the COO, leaned forward, ready to contribute. "Without a strategy, we risk implementing technologies in a disjointed manner, leading to inefficiencies and missed opportunities. A strategic approach ensures that all our technological efforts are aligned with our overall business goals and that we're making the best use of our resources."

Jim nodded in agreement. "Exactly. A cohesive strategy not only aligns our technological efforts with our business objectives but also prepares us to navigate the complexities and challenges of digital transformation. Now, let's delve into the key components of an effective digital transformation strategy."

He clicked to the next slide, which displayed **Key Components of a Digital Transformation Strategy**.

"The first component," Jim explained, "is **Assessing Current Capabilities**. This involves evaluating our existing technology, processes, and skills to identify strengths and areas for improvement. Leaders must understand where we currently stand to determine what changes are needed."

Janet Ross, the HR Director, raised a question. "How can we effectively assess our current capabilities?"

Jim appreciated Janet's inquiry. "Effectively assessing our current capabilities involves conducting thorough audits of our technology and processes, as well as gathering feedback from employees at all levels. Utilizing external consultants can also provide an objective perspective and identify gaps that we might overlook."

He continued to elaborate on the importance of assessing current capabilities.

"Next," Jim said, clicking to the next slide, "we have **Setting Clear Goals and Objectives**."

"Setting clear goals and objectives," he explained, "means defining what we want to achieve with our digital transformation efforts. These goals should be specific, measurable, achievable, relevant, and time-bound (SMART). Leaders must ensure that these goals are aligned with our overall business strategy."

Richard Shaw, the head of sales, nodded in agreement. "How can we ensure that our goals are aligned with our business strategy and realistic?"

"Ensuring alignment and realism," Jim replied, "involves

involving key stakeholders in the goal-setting process and conducting thorough market and competitive analysis. Regularly reviewing and adjusting our goals based on progress and feedback is also essential."

He continued to discuss the importance of setting clear goals and objectives.

"As executives," Jim concluded, "it's essential for us to develop a well-thought-out digital transformation strategy. By assessing our current capabilities and setting clear goals, we can create a roadmap for successful transformation that drives innovation and growth."

After Jim's presentation concluded, the room buzzed with determination as the team members discussed strategies for assessing their current capabilities and setting goals for their digital transformation. They now had a clearer understanding of the importance of a strategic approach to harnessing the power of technology.

As the meeting adjourned, Jim felt a sense of readiness. With a solid commitment to developing and implementing digital transformation strategies, he knew that his team was well-prepared to lead Cartwright Industries towards a future where technology was seamlessly integrated into every facet of their operations, driving success and innovation.

Leveraging Data Analytics

Jim Cartwright felt a surge of anticipation as he prepared to address the next critical aspect of their digital transformation journey—leveraging data analytics. He knew that understanding and utilizing data effectively could be a game-changer for Cartwright Industries, enabling smarter decisions and uncovering new opportunities.

"Good afternoon once again, everyone," Jim began, his voice filled with enthusiasm. "Today, we'll discuss how we can leverage data analytics to drive our digital transformation and achieve our strategic goals. Data is the new currency in today's business world, and our ability to harness its power will be crucial for our success."

He clicked the remote, and the slide titled **Leveraging Data Analytics: Turning Insights into Action** appeared on the screen.

"To start, let's consider why data analytics is so important," Jim continued. "What value does it bring to our organization?"

Paul Bennett, the COO, was quick to respond. "Data analytics allows us to make informed decisions based on real-time insights. It helps us identify trends, understand customer behavior, optimize operations, and predict future outcomes. Essentially, it transforms raw data into actionable intelligence."

Jim nodded in agreement. "Exactly. Now, let's delve into the key strategies for effectively leveraging data analytics."

He clicked to the next slide, which displayed **Key Strategies for Leveraging Data Analytics**.

"The first strategy," Jim explained, "is **Building a Data-Driven Culture**. This involves fostering an environment where data is valued and used consistently in decision-making processes. Leaders must champion the use of data and ensure that employees have the skills and tools to analyze and interpret data effectively."

Janet Ross, the HR Director, raised a question. "How can we cultivate a data-driven culture within our organization?"

Jim appreciated Janet's inquiry. "Cultivating a data-driven

culture involves providing regular training and development opportunities focused on data literacy. Leaders must also lead by example, using data to support their decisions and encouraging their teams to do the same. Recognizing and rewarding data-driven insights can further reinforce this culture."

He continued to elaborate on the importance of building a data-driven culture.

"Next," Jim said, clicking to the next slide, "we have **Implementing Advanced Analytics Tools**."

"Implementing advanced analytics tools," he explained, "means investing in the right technologies that can handle large volumes of data and perform sophisticated analyses. These tools should be user-friendly and integrated with our existing systems to ensure seamless data flow and accessibility."

Richard Shaw, the head of sales, nodded in agreement. "How can we choose the right analytics tools for our needs?"

"Choosing the right analytics tools," Jim replied, "involves assessing our specific needs and goals, consulting with experts, and considering scalability and ease of use. Leaders must ensure that the tools we select can grow with our organization and provide meaningful insights without being overly complex."

He continued to discuss the importance of implementing advanced analytics tools.

"As executives," Jim concluded, "it's essential for us to leverage data analytics to drive our digital transformation. By building a data-driven culture and implementing advanced analytics tools, we can turn insights into action and make informed decisions that propel our business forward."

After Jim's presentation concluded, the room buzzed with excitement as the team members discussed strategies for fostering a data-driven culture and selecting the right analytics tools. They now had a clearer understanding of how data analytics could empower them to achieve their goals and drive innovation.

As the meeting adjourned, Jim felt a renewed sense of purpose. With a solid commitment to leveraging data analytics, he knew that his team was well-prepared to lead Cartwright Industries towards a future where data-driven insights informed every decision, unlocking new opportunities and driving sustained success.

Cybersecurity Essentials

As Jim Cartwright transitioned to the next critical aspect of their digital transformation journey—cybersecurity essentials—he couldn't shake off the gravity of the topic. Cyber threats lurked around every corner, and protecting Cartwright Industries' digital assets was paramount to their success and reputation.

"Good afternoon, everyone," Jim began, his voice now carrying a tone of caution and vigilance. "Today, we'll discuss cybersecurity essentials—protecting our digital assets from ever-evolving threats. In the digital age, safeguarding our data and systems is non-negotiable."

He clicked the remote, and the slide titled **Cybersecurity Essentials: Safeguarding Our Digital Assets** appeared on the screen.

"To start, let's consider why cybersecurity is so critical," Jim continued. "What are the risks of neglecting cybersecurity, and how can they impact our organization?"

Paul Bennett, the COO, leaned forward, ready to contribute. "Neglecting cybersecurity can expose us to data breaches, financial losses, reputational damage, and legal liabilities. It can erode trust with our customers and partners and disrupt our operations. Essentially, it puts our entire business at risk."

Jim nodded in agreement. "Exactly. Now, let's delve into the key strategies for ensuring cybersecurity."

He clicked to the next slide, which displayed **Key Strategies for Cybersecurity**.

"The first strategy," Jim explained, "is **Creating a Culture of Security Awareness**. This involves educating and empowering our employees to recognize and respond to cyber threats effectively. Leaders must instill a sense of responsibility for cybersecurity in every individual and provide regular training on best practices and emerging threats."

Janet Ross, the HR Director, raised a question. "How can we ensure that our employees are aware of the latest cybersecurity threats and best practices?"

Jim appreciated Janet's inquiry. "Ensuring awareness," he replied, "involves providing ongoing training and resources, such as workshops, newsletters, and simulations. Leaders must also lead by example by following security protocols themselves and promoting a zero-tolerance policy for security lapses."

He continued to elaborate on the importance of creating a culture of security awareness.

"Next," Jim said, clicking to the next slide, "we have **Implementing Robust Security Measures**."

"Implementing robust security measures," he explained, "means deploying technologies and protocols to protect our digital assets from unauthorized access, malware, and other cyber threats. This includes measures such as firewalls, encryption, multi-factor authentication, and regular software updates."

Richard Shaw, the head of sales, nodded in agreement. "How can we ensure that our security measures are up to date and effective?"

"Ensuring effectiveness," Jim replied, "involves conducting regular security audits and assessments, as well as staying informed about the latest threats and vulnerabilities. Leaders must also collaborate with IT experts and external partners to implement industry best practices and continuously improve our security posture."

He continued to discuss the importance of implementing robust security measures.

"As executives," Jim concluded, "it's essential for us to prioritize cybersecurity to protect our digital assets and preserve trust with our stakeholders. By creating a culture of security awareness and implementing robust security measures, we can safeguard our organization against cyber threats and ensure our digital transformation journey is secure and successful."

After Jim's presentation concluded, the room buzzed with determination as the team members discussed strategies for fostering a culture of security awareness and enhancing their security measures. They now had a clearer understanding of the critical role that cybersecurity played in their digital transformation journey.

As the meeting adjourned, Jim felt a sense of reassurance. With a solid commitment to cybersecurity essentials, he knew that his team was well-prepared to navigate the complex and ever-evolving landscape of cyber threats, safeguarding Cartwright Industries' digital assets and reputation now and in the future.

Adopting Emerging Technologies

With the air charged with anticipation, Jim Cartwright approached the next crucial phase of their digital transformation journey—adopting emerging technologies. He knew that embracing innovation was key to staying ahead of the curve in a rapidly evolving landscape.

"Good afternoon once more, everyone," Jim began, his voice infused with excitement. "Today, we embark on a discussion about adopting emerging technologies—a pivotal step in our digital transformation journey. In a world of constant change, our ability to embrace innovation will determine our competitiveness and future success."

He clicked the remote, and the slide titled **Adopting Emerging Technologies: Staying Ahead of the Curve** appeared on the screen.

"To start, let's consider why adopting emerging technologies is so important," Jim continued. "What advantages do they offer, and how can they propel us forward?"

Paul Bennett, the COO, leaned forward, ready to contribute. "Emerging technologies offer the potential to revolutionize our operations, improve efficiency, enhance customer experiences, and drive innovation. By embracing these technologies early, we can gain a competitive edge and position ourselves as leaders in our industry."

Jim nodded in agreement. "Exactly. Now, let's delve into the key strategies for adopting emerging technologies."

He clicked to the next slide, which displayed **Key Strategies for Adopting Emerging Technologies**.

"The first strategy," Jim explained, "is **Staying Informed and Evaluating Opportunities**. This involves keeping abreast of the latest technological developments and assessing their potential impact on our business. Leaders must continuously monitor emerging trends, conduct pilot projects, and evaluate the feasibility and benefits of adopting new technologies."

Janet Ross, the HR Director, raised a question. "How can we ensure that we're making informed decisions about which emerging technologies to adopt?"

Jim appreciated Janet 's inquiry. "Ensuring informed decision-making," he replied, "involves gathering insights from industry experts, conducting thorough market research, and leveraging pilot projects and proofs of concept. Leaders must also involve key stakeholders from across the organization to ensure alignment with business goals and requirements."

He continued to elaborate on the importance of staying informed and evaluating opportunities.

"Next," Jim said, clicking to the next slide, "we have **Building Agile and Scalable Infrastructure**."

"Building agile and scalable infrastructure," he explained, "means investing in flexible and adaptable systems that can support the integration and deployment of emerging technologies. This includes cloud-based platforms, APIs, and microservices architectures that enable rapid innovation and scalability."

Richard Shaw, the head of sales, nodded in agreement. "How can we ensure that our infrastructure is agile and scalable?"

"Ensuring agility and scalability," Jim replied, "involves partnering with technology vendors that offer flexible solutions and adopting agile development methodologies. Leaders must also prioritize interoperability and standardization to facilitate seamless integration and scalability across our ecosystem."

He continued to discuss the importance of building agile and scalable infrastructure.

"As executives," Jim concluded, "it's essential for us to embrace emerging technologies to drive our digital transformation. By staying informed, evaluating opportunities, and building agile infrastructure, we can harness the power of innovation to stay ahead of the curve and achieve our strategic goals."

After Jim's presentation concluded, the room buzzed with excitement as the team members discussed strategies for staying informed about emerging technologies and building agile infrastructure. They now had a clearer understanding of how adopting emerging technologies could propel Cartwright Industries forward in their digital transformation journey.

As the meeting adjourned, Jim felt a sense of optimism. With a solid commitment to adopting emerging technologies, he knew that his team was well-prepared to embrace innovation and drive Cartwright Industries towards a future of success and leadership in their industry.

Case Studies in Digital Transformation

With a sense of eagerness, Jim Cartwright transitioned to the final part of their discussion—case studies in digital transformation. He knew that learning from real-world examples could provide invaluable insights and inspiration for their own journey.

"Good afternoon once again, everyone," Jim began, his voice now filled with anticipation. "Today, we'll explore case studies in digital transformation—examining real-world examples of organizations that have successfully embraced technology to drive innovation and achieve strategic goals. By studying these cases, we can gain valuable insights and lessons for our own journey."

He clicked the remote, and the slide titled **Case Studies in Digital Transformation: Learning from Success** appeared on the screen.

"To start, let's consider why studying case studies is so valuable," Jim continued. "What can we learn from the experiences of other organizations, and how can we apply those lessons to our own context?"

Paul Bennett, the COO, leaned forward, ready to contribute. "Studying case studies allows us to gain insights into best practices, challenges, and success factors in digital transformation. By understanding how other organizations have navigated similar journeys, we can identify strategies and tactics that are relevant to our own situation and adapt them to fit our needs."

Jim nodded in agreement. "Exactly. Now, let's delve into the key lessons from some notable case studies."

He clicked to the next slide, which displayed **Key Lessons from Case Studies**.

"The first case study," Jim explained, "is **Company X: Transforming Customer Experience**. Company X, a retail giant, embarked on a digital transformation journey to enhance its customer experience and stay competitive in the digital age. By leveraging data analytics, artificial intelligence, and omnichannel capabilities, Company X was able to personalize customer interactions, optimize inventory management, and drive sales growth."

Janet Ross, the HR Director, raised a question. "What were the key success factors for Company X in their digital transformation journey?"

Jim appreciated Janet's inquiry. "The key success factors," he replied, "included strong leadership commitment, a customer-centric approach, and a focus on agility and innovation. Company X also invested in employee training and collaboration to ensure alignment and adoption of new technologies across the organization."

He continued to elaborate on the lessons learned from Company X's digital transformation.

"Next," Jim said, clicking to the next slide, "we have **Company Y: Streamlining Operations with Automation**."

"Company Y, a manufacturing company," he explained, "implemented robotic process automation (RPA) to streamline its operations and improve efficiency. By automating repetitive and manual tasks, Company Y was able to reduce errors, increase productivity, and lower costs. This allowed them to reallocate resources to more strategic activities and accelerate their growth."

Richard Shaw, the head of sales, nodded in agreement. "What were the challenges that Company Y faced during their digital transformation?"

"The challenges," Jim replied, "included resistance to change, integration complexities, and ensuring data security and compliance. However, by addressing these challenges proactively and involving employees in the transformation process,

Company Y was able to overcome obstacles and achieve its goals."

He continued to discuss the lessons learned from Company Y's digital transformation.

"As executives," Jim concluded, "studying case studies provides us with valuable insights and inspiration for our own digital transformation journey. By learning from the experiences of others, we can identify strategies and tactics that will help us navigate challenges and achieve success."

After Jim's presentation concluded, the room buzzed with discussion as the team members analyzed the key lessons from the case studies and brainstormed how to apply them to their own situation. They now had a clearer understanding of the practical implications of digital transformation and were inspired to embark on their own journey of innovation and growth.

As the meeting adjourned, Jim felt a sense of excitement. With a solid foundation of knowledge and inspiration from real-world examples, he knew that his team was well-equipped to embark on their digital transformation journey with confidence and determination.

14

Chapter 14: Global Leadership

Leading in a Global Marketplace

As Jim Cartwright delved into the next chapter of their journey—global leadership—he understood the importance of navigating the complexities of a global marketplace. Leading in such an environment required a unique set of skills and strategies.

"Good afternoon, everyone," Jim began, his voice projecting authority and confidence. "Today, we'll explore global leadership—examining what it takes to lead successfully in a global marketplace. As our organization expands its reach and operations, it's essential for us to understand the nuances of global leadership and adapt our approach accordingly."

He clicked the remote, and the slide titled **Leading in a Global Marketplace: Navigating Cultural Diversity** appeared on the screen.

"To start," Jim continued, "let's consider why leading in a global marketplace is so important. What challenges and opportunities does it present, and how can we leverage them to our advantage?"

Paul Bennett, the COO, leaned forward, ready to contribute. "Leading in a global marketplace allows us to tap into new markets, access diverse talent pools, and capitalize on economies of scale. However, it also poses challenges such as cultural differences, regulatory complexities, and geopolitical risks. As global leaders, we must navigate these challenges effectively to ensure the success of our organization."

Jim nodded in agreement. "Exactly. Now, let's delve into the key strategies for leading in a global marketplace."

He clicked to the next slide, which displayed **Key Strategies for Global Leadership**.

"The first strategy," Jim explained, "is **Understanding Cultural Diversity**. This involves recognizing and respecting the cultural differences that exist across regions and countries. Leaders must adapt their communication styles, management approaches, and decision-making processes to accommodate diverse cultural norms and preferences."

Janet Ross, the HR Director, raised a question. "How can we ensure that we understand and respect cultural diversity in our global operations?"

Jim appreciated Janet's inquiry. "Ensuring understanding and respect," he replied, "involves investing in cultural intelligence training for employees at all levels of the organization. Leaders must also foster an inclusive and open-minded culture that values diversity and encourages cross-cultural collaboration. Regular engagement with local teams and stakeholders can further enhance cultural understanding and appreciation."

He continued to elaborate on the importance of understanding cultural diversity.

"Next," Jim said, clicking to the next slide, "we have **Building Cross-Cultural Teams**."

"Building cross-cultural teams," he explained, "means assembling teams with diverse backgrounds, perspectives, and experiences to leverage the benefits of cultural diversity. Leaders must promote collaboration, communication, and trust within these teams and ensure that everyone feels valued and included regardless of their cultural background."

Richard Shaw, the head of sales, nodded in agreement. "How can we effectively manage cross-cultural teams to maximize their potential?"

"Effectively managing cross-cultural teams," Jim replied, "involves establishing clear goals and expectations, providing cultural sensitivity training, and fostering a supportive and inclusive team culture. Leaders must also be mindful of potential conflicts and misunderstandings and proactively address them to maintain harmony and productivity within the team."

He continued to discuss the importance of building cross-cultural teams.

"As executives," Jim concluded, "leading in a global marketplace requires us to embrace cultural diversity and leverage it as a source of strength and innovation. By understanding cultural differences and building cross-cultural teams, we can effectively navigate the complexities of the global marketplace and drive success for our organization."

After Jim's presentation concluded, the room buzzed with discussion as the team members analyzed the key strategies for global leadership and shared their own experiences and insights. They now had a clearer understanding of the importance of cultural diversity in their global operations and were motivated to apply these strategies in their leadership roles.

As the meeting adjourned, Jim felt a sense of pride. With a solid commitment to understanding cultural diversity and building cross-cultural teams, he knew that his team was well-prepared to lead Cartwright Industries to new heights in the global marketplace, embracing diversity as a source of strength and competitive advantage.

Cross-Cultural Management

As Jim Cartwright continued his exploration of global leadership, he delved deeper into the intricacies of cross-cultural management. Leading in a global marketplace required not only understanding cultural diversity but also effectively managing it to foster collaboration and success.

"Good afternoon once more, everyone," Jim began, his voice resonating with authority. "In our discussion of global leadership, we now turn to the crucial aspect of cross-cultural management. As we expand our operations into diverse markets, it's essential for us to not only understand cultural differences but also manage them effectively to ensure the success of our organization."

He clicked the remote, and the slide titled **Cross-Cultural Management: Navigating Differences** appeared on the screen.

"To start," Jim continued, "let's consider why cross-cultural management is so important. What challenges do cultural differences present, and how can we address them to foster collaboration and synergy within our global teams?"

Paul Bennett, the COO, leaned forward, ready to contribute. "Cross-cultural management is essential because it helps us bridge the gap between diverse teams and align them towards common goals. Cultural differences can lead to misunderstandings, conflicts, and inefficiencies if not managed effectively. By understanding and respecting these differences, we can promote collaboration and synergy within our global teams."

Jim nodded in agreement. "Exactly. Now, let's delve into the key strategies for cross-cultural management."

He clicked to the next slide, which displayed **Key Strategies for Cross-Cultural Management**.

"The first strategy," Jim explained, "is **Promoting Open Communication**. This involves creating an environment where team members feel comfortable expressing their thoughts, ideas, and concerns openly, regardless of their cultural background. Leaders must encourage active listening, seek feedback, and foster a culture of transparency and trust."

Janet Ross, the HR Director, raised a question. "How can we promote open communication in our global teams?"

Jim appreciated Janet's inquiry. "Promoting open communication," he replied, "involves establishing clear communication channels, such as regular team meetings, virtual collaboration platforms, and feedback sessions. Leaders must also be accessible and approachable, encouraging team members to voice their opinions and contribute to discussions without fear of judgment or reprisal."

He continued to elaborate on the importance of promoting open communication.

"Next," Jim said, clicking to the next slide, "we have **Building Trust and Respect**."

"Building trust and respect," he explained, "means establishing strong relationships based on mutual understanding, empathy, and appreciation for diverse perspectives. Leaders must lead by example, demonstrating respect for cultural differences and building trust through their actions and decisions."

Richard Shaw, the head of sales, nodded in agreement. "How can we build trust and respect in our global teams?"

"Building trust and respect," Jim replied, "involves investing time and effort in relationship-building activities, such as team-building exercises, cultural immersion experiences, and cross-cultural training. Leaders must also recognize and celebrate cultural diversity, fostering an inclusive and supportive team culture where everyone feels valued and respected."

He continued to discuss the importance of building trust and respect.

"As executives," Jim concluded, "cross-cultural management is essential for fostering collaboration and success in a global marketplace. By promoting open communication, building trust and respect, and embracing cultural diversity, we can effectively manage our global teams and drive our organization towards its goals."

After Jim's presentation concluded, the room buzzed with discussion as the team members analyzed the key strategies for cross-cultural management and shared their own experiences and insights. They now had a clearer understanding of how to navigate cultural differences and promote collaboration within their global teams.

As the meeting adjourned, Jim felt a sense of satisfaction. With a solid commitment to promoting open communication and building trust and respect, he knew that his team was well-equipped to lead Cartwright Industries to success in the global marketplace, leveraging cultural diversity as a source of strength and innovation.

Navigating International Regulations

As Jim Cartwright delved deeper into the complexities of global leadership, he knew that navigating international regulations was paramount to success in the global marketplace. Leading in such an environment required a keen understanding of regulatory frameworks and compliance obligations across different regions.

"Good afternoon once more, everyone," Jim began, his voice projecting authority and gravitas. "In our exploration of global leadership, we now turn to the critical aspect of navigating international regulations. As we expand our operations into diverse markets, it's essential for us to understand and comply with the regulatory requirements of each region to ensure the success and sustainability of our organization."

He clicked the remote, and the slide titled **Navigating International Regulations: Ensuring Compliance** appeared on the screen.

"To start," Jim continued, "let's consider why navigating international regulations is so important. What challenges do regulatory differences present, and how can we address them to ensure compliance and mitigate risks?"

Paul Bennett, the COO, leaned forward, ready to contribute. "Navigating international regulations is crucial because it helps us avoid legal and financial repercussions and maintain our reputation and credibility in the global marketplace. Regulatory differences can lead to compliance failures, fines, and legal disputes if not managed effectively. By understanding and adhering to the regulatory requirements of each region, we can ensure compliance and mitigate risks effectively."

Jim nodded in agreement. "Exactly. Now, let's delve into the key strategies for navigating international regulations."

He clicked to the next slide, which displayed **Key Strategies for Navigating International Regulations**.

"The first strategy," Jim explained, "is **Conducting Comprehensive Regulatory Research**. This involves thoroughly researching the regulatory frameworks and compliance requirements of each region where we operate or plan to expand. Leaders must identify relevant laws, regulations, and industry standards and assess their implications for our operations and business activities."

Janet Ross, the HR Director, raised a question. "How can we ensure that we stay up-to-date with the latest regulatory changes and developments?"

Jim appreciated Janet's inquiry. "Staying up-to-date," he replied, "involves establishing robust monitoring mechanisms, such as subscribing to regulatory updates, engaging with legal experts and industry associations, and participating in relevant training and workshops. Leaders must also foster a culture of compliance awareness and accountability across the organization to ensure that regulatory requirements are understood and followed at all levels."

He continued to elaborate on the importance of conducting comprehensive regulatory research.

"Next," Jim said, clicking to the next slide, "we have **Establishing a Compliance Management System**."

"Establishing a compliance management system," he explained, "means implementing policies, procedures, and controls to ensure that our operations and business activities comply with applicable laws and regulations. Leaders must designate compliance officers, establish reporting mechanisms, and conduct regular audits and assessments to monitor and enforce compliance effectively."

Richard Shaw, the head of sales, nodded in agreement. "How can we ensure that our compliance management system is effective and robust?"

"Ensuring effectiveness and robustness," Jim replied, "involves prioritizing risk assessment and mitigation, fostering a culture of ethics and integrity, and providing regular training and resources to employees. Leaders must also collaborate with legal experts and regulatory authorities to address compliance challenges and stay ahead of regulatory developments."

He continued to discuss the importance of establishing a compliance management system.

"As executives," Jim concluded, "navigating international regulations is essential for ensuring the success and sustainability of our organization in the global marketplace. By conducting comprehensive regulatory research, establishing a compliance management system, and fostering a culture of compliance awareness, we can navigate regulatory complexities effectively and mitigate risks proactively."

After Jim's presentation concluded, the room buzzed with discussion as the team members analyzed the key strategies for navigating international regulations and shared their own experiences and insights. They now had a clearer understanding of the importance of compliance in their global operations and were motivated to ensure that Cartwright Industries remained compliant in all regions where they operated.

As the meeting adjourned, Jim felt a sense of reassurance. With a solid commitment to navigating international regulations, he knew that his team was well-equipped to lead Cartwright Industries to success in the global marketplace, ensuring compliance and mitigating risks effectively across diverse regions and jurisdictions.

Global Expansion Strategies

As Jim Cartwright delved deeper into the realm of global leadership, he recognized the importance of formulating effective strategies for global expansion. Leading in a global marketplace required a clear vision and strategic approach to penetrate new markets and capitalize on growth opportunities.

"Good afternoon once more, everyone," Jim began, his voice exuding confidence and determination. "In our exploration of global leadership, we now shift our focus to the pivotal aspect of global expansion strategies. As we aspire to grow our footprint in diverse markets, it's essential for us to develop comprehensive strategies that enable us to enter new regions, seize opportunities, and drive sustainable growth for our organization."

He clicked the remote, and the slide titled **Global Expansion Strategies: Seizing Growth Opportunities** appeared on the screen.

"To start," Jim continued, "let's consider why developing global expansion strategies is so important. What challenges and opportunities do global markets present, and how can we leverage them to our advantage?"

Paul Bennett, the COO, leaned forward, ready to contribute. "Developing global expansion strategies is crucial because it allows us to tap into new markets, access untapped customer segments, and diversify our revenue streams. However, it also poses challenges such as cultural differences, regulatory complexities, and competitive landscapes. By developing comprehensive strategies, we can navigate these challenges effectively and capitalize on growth opportunities."

Jim nodded in agreement. "Exactly. Now, let's delve into the key strategies for global expansion."

He clicked to the next slide, which displayed **Key Strategies for Global Expansion**.

"The first strategy," Jim explained, "is **Market Research and Analysis**. This involves conducting thorough research and analysis to identify attractive markets, assess market potential, and understand customer needs and preferences. Leaders must analyze demographic trends, economic indicators, and competitive landscapes to inform their expansion decisions."

Janet Ross, the HR Director, raised a question. "How can we ensure that our market research is accurate and reliable?"

Jim appreciated Janet's inquiry. "Ensuring accuracy and reliability," he replied, "involves leveraging a combination of quantitative and qualitative research methods, such as surveys, focus groups, and data analytics. Leaders must also engage with local experts and industry insiders to gain insights into market dynamics and trends. Additionally, conducting pilot projects and market tests can help validate assumptions and reduce risks associated with market entry."

He continued to elaborate on the importance of market research and analysis.

"Next," Jim said, clicking to the next slide, "we have **Strate-**

gic Partnerships and Alliances."

"Forming strategic partnerships and alliances," he explained, "means collaborating with local businesses, distributors, and suppliers to leverage their expertise, networks, and resources. Leaders must identify potential partners that share their values and strategic objectives and negotiate mutually beneficial agreements that enable them to expand their reach and market presence effectively."

Richard Shaw, the head of sales, nodded in agreement. "How can we identify and evaluate potential partners for strategic alliances?"

"Identifying and evaluating partners," Jim replied, "involves conducting due diligence, assessing their reputation, capabilities, and compatibility with our organization. Leaders must also establish clear objectives, roles, and responsibilities for each partner and establish mechanisms for communication, collaboration, and performance measurement."

He continued to discuss the importance of strategic partnerships and alliances.

"As executives," Jim concluded, "developing global expansion strategies is essential for driving sustainable growth and success in the global marketplace. By conducting market research and analysis, forming strategic partnerships and alliances, and leveraging local expertise, we can penetrate new markets and capitalize on growth opportunities effectively."

After Jim's presentation concluded, the room buzzed with discussion as the team members analyzed the key strategies for global expansion and shared their own experiences and insights. They now had a clearer understanding of how to formulate comprehensive strategies for entering new markets and were motivated to execute their expansion plans with confidence and determination.

As the meeting adjourned, Jim felt a sense of excitement. With a solid commitment to global expansion strategies, he knew that his team was well-equipped to lead Cartwright Industries to success in the global marketplace, seizing growth opportunities and driving sustainable growth across diverse regions and markets.

Managing Global Teams

Jim Cartwright's journey into global leadership took him to the critical aspect of managing global teams. He understood that effective leadership in a global context required the ability to lead and coordinate teams across different time zones, cultures, and geographies.

"Good afternoon once more, everyone," Jim began, his voice carrying the weight of experience. "In our exploration of global leadership, we now turn to the crucial aspect of managing global teams. As our organization expands its reach into diverse markets, it's essential for us to foster collaboration, communication, and cohesion among our teams across the globe."

He clicked the remote, and the slide titled **Managing Global Teams: Fostering Collaboration** appeared on the screen.

"To start," Jim continued, "let's consider why managing global teams is so important. What challenges do dispersed teams present, and how can we address them to ensure productivity and effectiveness?"

Paul Bennett, the COO, nodded in agreement. "Managing global teams is essential because it allows us to leverage diverse talent pools, access local expertise, and adapt to local market conditions. However, it also poses challenges such as communication barriers, coordination complexities, and cultural differences. By implementing effective strategies for managing global teams, we can overcome these challenges and maximize the potential of our teams."

Jim nodded in agreement. "Exactly. Now, let's delve into the key strategies for managing global teams."

He clicked to the next slide, which displayed **Key Strategies for Managing Global Teams**.

"The first strategy," Jim explained, "is **Establishing Clear Communication Channels**. This involves setting up communication platforms and protocols that enable seamless communication and information sharing across global teams. Leaders must ensure that team members have access to the necessary tools and resources for effective communication, such as video conferencing, collaboration software, and project management tools."

Janet Ross, the HR Director, raised a question. "How can we ensure that communication remains effective across different time zones and cultures?"

Jim appreciated Janet's inquiry. "Ensuring effective communication," he replied, "involves establishing norms and expectations for communication, such as designated meeting times, response times, and communication preferences. Leaders must also be mindful of cultural differences in communication styles and adapt their approach accordingly to ensure clarity and understanding."

He continued to elaborate on the importance of clear communication channels.

"Next," Jim said, clicking to the next slide, "we have **Promoting Collaboration and Team Building**."

"Promoting collaboration and team building," he explained, "means creating opportunities for team members to connect, collaborate, and build relationships across geographical boundaries. Leaders must organize virtual team-building activities, cross-cultural training sessions, and knowledge-sharing initiatives to foster a sense of belonging and camaraderie among global teams."

Richard Shaw, the head of sales, nodded in agreement. "How can we ensure that global teams remain aligned with the organization's goals and objectives?"

"Ensuring alignment," Jim replied, "involves communicating the organization's vision, mission, and strategic priorities clearly and consistently across global teams. Leaders must also provide regular updates on organizational performance, share success stories and best practices, and solicit feedback from team members to ensure that everyone is working towards common goals."

He continued to discuss the importance of promoting collaboration and alignment among global teams.

"As executives," Jim concluded, "managing global teams is essential for driving innovation, efficiency, and competitiveness in the global marketplace. By establishing clear communication channels, promoting collaboration and team building, and ensuring alignment with organizational goals, we can harness the full potential of our global teams and achieve success in our global endeavors."

After Jim's presentation concluded, the room buzzed with discussion as the team members analyzed the key strategies for managing global teams and shared their own experiences and insights. They now had a clearer understanding of how to effectively lead and coordinate teams across different regions and were motivated to apply these strategies in their global leadership roles.

As the meeting adjourned, Jim felt a sense of optimism. With a solid commitment to managing global teams, he knew that his team was well-equipped to navigate the complexities of global leadership and drive Cartwright Industries towards continued success in the global marketplace.

Learning from Global Leaders

Jim Cartwright's exploration of global leadership took him to the final subpoint: learning from global leaders. He understood the value of studying successful leaders who had navigated the complexities of the global marketplace and gleaned insights that could inform his own leadership approach.

"Good afternoon once more, everyone," Jim began, his voice resonating with curiosity and eagerness. "In our journey of understanding global leadership, we now shift our focus to the invaluable aspect of learning from global leaders. As we strive to excel in the global marketplace, it's essential for us to draw inspiration and insights from leaders who have successfully led organizations on the global stage."

He clicked the remote, and the slide titled **Learning from Global Leaders: Extracting Insights** appeared on the screen.

"To start," Jim continued, "let's consider why learning from global leaders is so important. What lessons can we extract from their experiences, and how can we apply them to our own leadership journey?"

Paul Bennett, the COO, nodded in agreement. "Learning

from global leaders is essential because it allows us to gain insights into effective leadership practices, global market trends, and innovative strategies. By studying their successes and failures, we can identify best practices, avoid common pitfalls, and refine our own leadership approach to achieve greater success in the global marketplace."

Jim nodded in agreement. "Exactly. Now, let's delve into the key strategies for learning from global leaders."

He clicked to the next slide, which displayed **Key Strategies for Learning from Global Leaders**.

"The first strategy," Jim explained, "is **Studying Case Studies and Success Stories**. This involves analyzing case studies and success stories of prominent global leaders and organizations to understand their leadership philosophies, strategic decisions, and business outcomes. Leaders must extract key insights and lessons learned from these case studies and apply them to their own leadership practices."

Janet Ross, the HR Director, raised a question. "How can we ensure that we learn from a diverse range of global leaders and perspectives?"

Jim appreciated Janet 's inquiry. "Ensuring diversity," he replied, "involves studying case studies and success stories from a variety of industries, regions, and cultural contexts. Leaders must seek out perspectives from different sectors and geographies to gain a comprehensive understanding of global leadership practices and trends."

He continued to elaborate on the importance of studying case studies and success stories.

"Next," Jim said, clicking to the next slide, "we have **Seeking Mentorship and Guidance**."

"Seeking mentorship and guidance," he explained, "means

connecting with experienced global leaders who can provide advice, guidance, and mentorship based on their own experiences and insights. Leaders must seek out mentors who have successfully navigated the challenges of global leadership and can offer valuable perspectives and support."

Richard Shaw, the head of sales, nodded in agreement. "How can we identify and approach potential mentors for guidance?"

"Identifying mentors," Jim replied, "involves networking, attending industry events, and reaching out to leaders whose experiences align with our own leadership goals and aspirations. Leaders must approach potential mentors with humility, respect, and a genuine desire to learn, and be open to receiving feedback and guidance from them."

He continued to discuss the importance of seeking mentorship and guidance.

"As executives," Jim concluded, "learning from global leaders is essential for honing our leadership skills, expanding our perspectives, and staying ahead of the curve in the global marketplace. By studying case studies and success stories, seeking mentorship and guidance, and applying key insights to our own leadership practices, we can continue to grow and excel as global leaders."

After Jim's presentation concluded, the room buzzed with discussion as the team members analyzed the key strategies for learning from global leaders and shared their own experiences and insights. They now had a clearer understanding of how to leverage the experiences of global leaders to enhance their own leadership journey and drive Cartwright Industries towards continued success in the global marketplace.

As the meeting adjourned, Jim felt a sense of excitement.

With a solid commitment to learning from global leaders, he knew that his team was well-equipped to navigate the complexities of global leadership and drive Cartwright Industries towards continued growth and prosperity on the global stage.

15

Chapter 15: Personal Development and Work-Life Balance

Continuous Learning and Education

J im Cartwright, in his pursuit of excellence in leadership, now turned his attention to the crucial aspect of personal development and work-life balance. He recognized that continuous learning and education were fundamental to growth, both professionally and personally.

"Good afternoon once more, everyone," Jim began, his voice infused with a sense of introspection and determination. "In our exploration of leadership, we now delve into the vital topic of personal development and work-life balance. As leaders, it's imperative for us to prioritize our own growth and well-being, ensuring that we continue to learn, evolve, and thrive in both our professional and personal lives."

He clicked the remote, and the slide titled **Continuous Learning and Education: Investing in Growth** appeared on the screen.

"To start," Jim continued, "let's consider why continuous learning and education are so crucial. What benefits do they offer, and how can they contribute to our overall development and fulfillment?"

Paul Bennett, the COO, nodded thoughtfully. "Continuous learning and education are essential because they enable us to stay relevant, adapt to change, and expand our perspectives. By investing in our own growth, we not only enhance our skills and knowledge but also increase our capacity to lead effectively and inspire others."

Jim nodded in agreement. "Exactly. Now, let's delve into the key strategies for continuous learning and education."

He clicked to the next slide, which displayed **Key Strategies for Continuous Learning and Education**.

"The first strategy," Jim explained, "is **Setting Learning Goals**. This involves identifying areas for personal and professional development and setting specific, measurable goals to guide our learning journey. Whether it's acquiring new skills, pursuing advanced degrees, or exploring new interests, setting clear goals helps us stay focused and motivated."

Janet Ross, the HR Director, raised a question. "How can we ensure that we make time for learning amidst our busy schedules?"

Jim appreciated Janet's inquiry. "Making time for learning," he replied, "involves prioritizing and scheduling dedicated time for self-improvement activities. Leaders must carve out time in their schedules for reading, attending seminars, taking courses, or engaging in other learning opportunities. By treating learning as a priority, we can ensure that we continue to grow and develop despite our busy schedules."

He continued to elaborate on the importance of setting

learning goals.

"Next," Jim said, clicking to the next slide, "we have **Embracing Lifelong Learning**."

"Embracing lifelong learning," he explained, "means adopting a growth mindset and committing to continuous improvement throughout our lives. Leaders must view challenges as opportunities for growth, seek out feedback and constructive criticism, and embrace new experiences and perspectives. By cultivating a habit of lifelong learning, we can remain adaptable, resilient, and innovative in the face of change."

Richard Shaw, the head of sales, nodded in agreement. "How can we foster a culture of lifelong learning within our organization?"

"Fostering a culture of lifelong learning," Jim replied, "involves leading by example and creating opportunities for learning and development for our teams. Leaders must encourage curiosity, experimentation, and knowledge-sharing among team members, and provide resources and support for their continuous growth and development. By prioritizing learning at all levels of the organization, we can create a culture of excellence and innovation that drives our collective success."

He continued to discuss the importance of embracing lifelong learning.

"As executives," Jim concluded, "continuous learning and education are essential for our growth, fulfillment, and effectiveness as leaders. By setting learning goals, embracing lifelong learning, and fostering a culture of continuous improvement within our organization, we can ensure that we continue to evolve and thrive in both our professional and personal lives."

After Jim's presentation concluded, the room buzzed with discussion as the team members analyzed the key strategies for continuous learning and education and shared their own experiences and insights. They now had a clearer understanding of how to prioritize their own growth and well-being amidst their demanding roles as leaders, and were motivated to embark on their own learning journeys with renewed enthusiasm and commitment.

As the meeting adjourned, Jim felt a sense of optimism. With a solid commitment to continuous learning and education, he knew that he and his team were well-equipped to navigate the complexities of leadership and achieve their goals while maintaining a healthy work-life balance.

Time Management Techniques

Jim Cartwright, in his quest for personal development and work-life balance, now shifted his focus to the critical aspect of time management techniques. He understood that effective time management was essential for maximizing productivity and achieving a harmonious balance between work and personal life.

"Good afternoon once more, everyone," Jim began, his voice tinged with determination and practicality. "In our exploration of personal development and work-life balance, we now delve into the essential topic of time management techniques. As leaders, it's crucial for us to optimize our time and energy to fulfill our responsibilities effectively while also prioritizing our well-being and personal pursuits."

He clicked the remote, and the slide titled **Time Management Techniques: Maximizing Productivity** appeared on the screen.

"To start," Jim continued, "let's consider why time management techniques are so vital. What benefits do they offer, and how can they help us achieve a more balanced and fulfilling life?"

Paul Bennett, the COO, leaned forward attentively. "Time management techniques are crucial because they enable us to prioritize tasks, minimize distractions, and make the most of our limited time and energy. By mastering time management, we can increase our productivity, reduce stress, and create space for activities that nourish our personal well-being."

Jim nodded in agreement. "Exactly. Now, let's delve into the key strategies for effective time management."

He clicked to the next slide, which displayed **Key Time Management Techniques**.

"The first technique," Jim explained, "is **Prioritizing Tasks**. This involves identifying tasks based on their importance and urgency and allocating time and resources accordingly. Leaders must distinguish between tasks that are essential for achieving their goals and those that can be delegated, deferred, or eliminated to focus on what truly matters."

Janet Ross, the HR Director, raised a question. "How can we determine which tasks to prioritize amidst competing demands?"

Jim appreciated Janet 's inquiry. "Determining task priorities," he replied, "involves using frameworks such as the Eisenhower Matrix or the ABCDE method to categorize tasks based on their significance and deadlines. Leaders must also consider their long-term goals and values when prioritizing tasks, ensuring alignment with their overall vision and objectives."

He continued to elaborate on the importance of prioritizing tasks.

"Next," Jim said, clicking to the next slide, "we have **Setting Boundaries and Limits.**"

"Setting boundaries and limits," he explained, "means establishing clear guidelines for how we allocate our time and energy and enforcing them rigorously. Leaders must learn to say no to non-essential commitments, delegate tasks effectively, and set realistic expectations for themselves and others. By setting boundaries, we can prevent burnout, maintain work-life balance, and preserve our overall well-being."

Richard Shaw, the head of sales, nodded in agreement. "How can we ensure that we stick to our boundaries amidst pressure and demands?"

"Sticking to boundaries," Jim replied, "involves practicing self-discipline, communicating boundaries assertively, and seeking support from colleagues and loved ones. Leaders must also regularly review and adjust their boundaries based on changing circumstances and priorities, ensuring that they remain aligned with their needs and goals."

He continued to discuss the importance of setting boundaries and limits.

"As executives," Jim concluded, "time management techniques are essential for optimizing our productivity and achieving a more balanced and fulfilling life. By prioritizing tasks, setting boundaries, and managing our time effectively, we can create space for both our professional responsibilities and personal pursuits, leading to greater satisfaction and success in all aspects of our lives."

After Jim's presentation concluded, the room buzzed with

discussion as the team members analyzed the key time management techniques and shared their own experiences and insights. They now had a clearer understanding of how to optimize their time and energy to achieve their goals while maintaining a healthy work-life balance, and were motivated to implement these techniques in their daily lives with renewed focus and determination.

As the meeting adjourned, Jim felt a sense of empowerment. With a solid commitment to time management techniques, he knew that he and his team were well-equipped to navigate the complexities of leadership and lead fulfilling lives both professionally and personally.

Maintaining Physical and Mental Health

Jim Cartwright, in his exploration of personal development and work-life balance, now turned his attention to the crucial aspect of maintaining physical and mental health. He understood that prioritizing well-being was essential for sustaining long-term success and fulfillment in both professional and personal life.

"Good afternoon once more, everyone," Jim began, his tone compassionate yet resolute. "In our journey of self-discovery and balance, we now focus on the pivotal topic of maintaining physical and mental health. As leaders, it's imperative for us to prioritize our well-being, ensuring that we nurture our bodies and minds to thrive in all aspects of our lives."

He clicked the remote, and the slide titled **Maintaining Physical and Mental Health: Nurturing Well-being** appeared on the screen.

"To start," Jim continued, "let's consider why maintaining

physical and mental health is so vital. What benefits does it offer, and how can it contribute to our overall success and happiness?"

Paul Bennett, the COO, nodded thoughtfully. "Maintaining physical and mental health is crucial because it enables us to perform at our best, manage stress effectively, and sustain our energy and motivation over the long term. By prioritizing well-being, we not only enhance our quality of life but also increase our resilience and capacity to lead effectively."

Jim nodded in agreement. "Exactly. Now, let's delve into the key strategies for maintaining physical and mental health."

He clicked to the next slide, which displayed **Key Strategies for Well-being**.

"The first strategy," Jim explained, "is **Caring for the Body**. This involves prioritizing activities that promote physical health, such as regular exercise, nutritious eating, adequate sleep, and preventive healthcare. Leaders must make time for physical activity, prioritize nutritious meals, and establish healthy sleep habits to support their overall well-being."

Janet Ross, the HR Director, raised a question. "How can we ensure that we prioritize our physical health amidst busy schedules and demands?"

Jim appreciated Janet 's inquiry. "Prioritizing physical health," he replied, "involves making conscious choices and setting boundaries to ensure that we allocate time and energy to self-care activities. Leaders must view physical health as a non-negotiable aspect of their routine and incorporate it into their daily schedule, even amidst pressing responsibilities."

He continued to elaborate on the importance of caring for the body.

"Next," Jim said, clicking to the next slide, "we have **Nurtur-**

ing Mental Health."

"Nurturing mental health," he explained, "means prioritizing activities that support emotional well-being, such as stress management, relaxation techniques, mindfulness practices, and seeking support when needed. Leaders must recognize the importance of mental health and proactively address stressors, cultivate resilience, and seek professional help if necessary to maintain optimal mental well-being."

Richard Shaw, the head of sales, nodded in agreement. "How can we create a supportive culture that prioritizes mental health within our organization?"

"Creating a supportive culture," Jim replied, "involves fostering open communication, destigmatizing mental health issues, and providing resources and support for employees to address their mental well-being. Leaders must lead by example, prioritize self-care, and encourage their teams to prioritize their own mental health, creating a culture of trust, empathy, and support within the organization."

He continued to discuss the importance of nurturing mental health.

"As executives," Jim concluded, "maintaining physical and mental health is essential for sustaining our well-being, performance, and fulfillment as leaders. By caring for our bodies and minds, we can increase our resilience, creativity, and effectiveness, leading to greater success and happiness in all aspects of our lives."

After Jim's presentation concluded, the room buzzed with discussion as the team members analyzed the key strategies for maintaining physical and mental health and shared their own experiences and insights. They now had a clearer understanding of how to prioritize their well-being amidst their demanding roles as leaders, and were motivated to incorporate these strategies into their daily lives with renewed commitment and intention.

As the meeting adjourned, Jim felt a sense of gratitude. With a solid commitment to maintaining physical and mental health, he knew that he and his team were well-equipped to navigate the challenges of leadership with resilience, vitality, and fulfillment.

Balancing Work and Personal Life

Jim Cartwright, in his pursuit of personal development and work-life balance, now directed his attention to the delicate art of balancing work and personal life. He understood that achieving harmony between professional responsibilities and personal pursuits was essential for sustained well-being and fulfillment.

"Good afternoon once more, everyone," Jim began, his voice reflective yet determined. "In our exploration of personal development and work-life balance, we now delve into the critical topic of balancing work and personal life. As leaders, it's crucial for us to cultivate a harmonious integration of our professional responsibilities and personal pursuits, ensuring that we lead fulfilling lives both inside and outside of the workplace."

He clicked the remote, and the slide titled **Balancing Work and Personal Life: Cultivating Harmony** appeared on the screen.

"To start," Jim continued, "let's consider why balancing work and personal life is so essential. What benefits does it offer, and how can it contribute to our overall well-being and success?"

Paul Bennett, the COO, nodded in agreement. "Balancing work and personal life is essential because it allows us to nurture our relationships, pursue our passions, and recharge our energy outside of work. By achieving a sense of harmony between our professional and personal lives, we can enhance our satisfaction, resilience, and effectiveness as leaders."

Jim nodded in agreement. "Exactly. Now, let's delve into the key strategies for balancing work and personal life."

He clicked to the next slide, which displayed **Key Strategies for Balance**.

"The first strategy," Jim explained, "is **Setting Boundaries**. This involves establishing clear boundaries between work and personal life and honoring them consistently. Leaders must define specific times for work-related activities and leisure pursuits, and refrain from allowing work to encroach upon personal time."

Janet Ross, the HR Director, raised a question. "How can we ensure that we maintain boundaries amidst the pressures and demands of our roles?"

Jim appreciated Janet's inquiry. "Maintaining boundaries," he replied, "involves communicating expectations clearly with colleagues and loved ones, delegating tasks effectively, and resisting the temptation to constantly check email or respond to work-related matters outside of designated work hours. Leaders must prioritize self-care and respect their own boundaries to set a positive example for their teams."

He continued to elaborate on the importance of setting boundaries.

"Next," Jim said, clicking to the next slide, "we have **Prioritizing Personal Time**."

"Prioritizing personal time," he explained, "means making deliberate choices to allocate time and energy to activities that nourish our personal well-being and fulfillment. Leaders must schedule regular breaks, engage in hobbies and interests, and spend quality time with family and friends to recharge and rejuvenate outside of work."

Richard Shaw, the head of sales, nodded in agreement. "How can we ensure that we prioritize personal time amidst busy schedules and competing demands?"

"Prioritizing personal time," Jim replied, "involves making conscious decisions to carve out time for self-care and leisure activities, even amidst pressing responsibilities. Leaders must view personal time as essential for their overall well-being and effectiveness, and proactively schedule it into their calendars to ensure that it receives the attention it deserves."

He continued to discuss the importance of prioritizing personal time.

"As executives," Jim concluded, "balancing work and personal life is essential for sustaining our well-being, satisfaction, and effectiveness as leaders. By setting boundaries, prioritizing personal time, and integrating work and personal life in a harmonious way, we can achieve greater fulfillment and success in all aspects of our lives."

After Jim's presentation concluded, the room buzzed with discussion as the team members analyzed the key strategies for balancing work and personal life and shared their own experiences and insights. They now had a clearer understanding of how to cultivate harmony between their professional responsibilities and personal pursuits, and were motivated to implement these strategies into their daily lives with renewed intention and commitment.

As the meeting adjourned, Jim felt a sense of optimism. With a solid commitment to balancing work and personal life, he knew that he and his team were well-equipped to navigate the complexities of leadership with resilience, vitality, and fulfillment.

Networking and Mentorship

Jim Cartwright, in his exploration of personal development and work-life balance, now focused on the transformative power of networking and mentorship. He understood that building meaningful connections and seeking guidance from experienced mentors were essential for personal growth and professional advancement.

"Good afternoon once more, everyone," Jim began, his voice resonating with enthusiasm and purpose. "In our journey towards personal development and work-life balance, we now delve into the invaluable topic of networking and mentorship. As leaders, it's crucial for us to cultivate strong relationships and seek guidance from mentors who can help us navigate the complexities of leadership and achieve our goals."

He clicked the remote, and the slide titled **Networking and Mentorship: Building Connections** appeared on the screen.

"To start," Jim continued, "let's consider why networking and mentorship are so vital. What benefits do they offer, and how can they contribute to our growth and success?"

Paul Bennett, the COO, nodded thoughtfully. "Networking and mentorship are essential because they provide opportunities for learning, collaboration, and personal growth. By connecting with peers and seeking guidance from experienced mentors, we can gain valuable insights, expand our perspectives, and advance our careers."

Jim nodded in agreement. "Exactly. Now, let's delve into the key strategies for networking and mentorship."

He clicked to the next slide, which displayed **Key Strategies for Building Connections**.

"The first strategy," Jim explained, "is **Building Genuine Relationships**. This involves approaching networking with authenticity, sincerity, and a genuine interest in others. Leaders must take the time to get to know their colleagues, peers, and industry contacts on a personal level, and seek to establish meaningful connections based on mutual trust and respect."

Janet Ross, the HR Director, raised a question. "How can we build genuine relationships in a professional context?"

Jim appreciated Janet 's inquiry. "Building genuine relationships," he replied, "involves listening actively, showing empathy, and being willing to offer support and assistance to others without expecting anything in return. Leaders must approach networking as an opportunity to add value to others' lives and build long-lasting connections based on trust and reciprocity."

He continued to elaborate on the importance of building genuine relationships.

"Next," Jim said, clicking to the next slide, "we have **Seeking Mentorship**."

"Seeking mentorship," he explained, "means identifying experienced professionals who can offer guidance, advice, and support as we navigate our careers and personal development. Leaders must be proactive in seeking out mentors who possess the knowledge, skills, and experience that align with their goals and aspirations, and be open to learning from their insights and perspectives."

Richard Shaw, the head of sales, nodded in agreement. "How can we find mentors who are the right fit for us?"

"Finding mentors," Jim replied, "involves reaching out to colleagues, peers, and industry contacts who inspire us and possess the expertise and experience we seek. Leaders must be proactive in networking and expressing their interest in mentorship opportunities, and be willing to invest time and effort in nurturing relationships with potential mentors."

He continued to discuss the importance of seeking mentorship.

"As executives," Jim concluded, "networking and mentorship are essential for our growth, development, and success as leaders. By building genuine relationships and seeking guidance from experienced mentors, we can expand our knowledge, skills, and perspectives, and achieve greater fulfillment and effectiveness in our personal and professional lives."

After Jim's presentation concluded, the room buzzed with discussion as the team members analyzed the key strategies for networking and mentorship and shared their own experiences and insights. They now had a clearer understanding of how to cultivate strong relationships and seek guidance from mentors, and were motivated to leverage these strategies to accelerate their personal and professional growth with renewed enthusiasm and determination.

As the meeting adjourned, Jim felt a sense of excitement. With a solid commitment to networking and mentorship, he knew that he and his team were well-equipped to cultivate meaningful connections, seek valuable guidance, and achieve their goals with confidence and clarity.

Setting Personal Goals and Milestones

Jim Cartwright, in his pursuit of personal development and work-life balance, now turned his attention to the importance of setting personal goals and milestones. He understood that having clear objectives and actionable steps was essential for staying focused and motivated in both professional and personal endeavors.

"Good afternoon once more, everyone," Jim began, his voice filled with determination and purpose. "In our exploration of personal development and work-life balance, we now delve into the pivotal topic of setting personal goals and milestones. As leaders, it's crucial for us to establish clear objectives and actionable steps to guide our journey towards success and fulfillment."

He clicked the remote, and the slide titled **Setting Personal Goals and Milestones: Charting Your Path** appeared on the screen.

"To start," Jim continued, "let's consider why setting personal goals and milestones is so vital. What benefits do they offer, and how can they contribute to our growth and happiness?"

Paul Bennett, the COO, leaned forward attentively. "Setting personal goals and milestones is essential because it provides direction, focus, and motivation for our actions. By defining clear objectives and actionable steps, we can measure our progress, overcome obstacles, and achieve our aspirations with confidence and clarity."

Jim nodded in agreement. "Exactly. Now, let's delve into the key strategies for setting personal goals and milestones."

He clicked to the next slide, which displayed **Key Strategies for Charting Your Path**.

"The first strategy," Jim explained, "is **Clarifying Your Vision**. This involves reflecting on your values, passions, and aspirations to identify what matters most to you and what you want to achieve in the long term. Leaders must take the time to envision their ideal future and articulate their goals with clarity and specificity."

Janet Ross, the HR Director, raised a question. "How can we ensure that our personal goals align with our values and aspirations?"

Jim appreciated Janet 's inquiry. "Aligning personal goals with values," he replied, "involves examining your core beliefs, priorities, and desires to ensure that your goals are meaningful and fulfilling. Leaders must consider how their goals contribute to their overall well-being and fulfillment, and be willing to adjust them as they evolve and grow."

He continued to elaborate on the importance of clarifying the vision.

"Next," Jim said, clicking to the next slide, "we have **Setting SMART Goals**."

"Setting SMART goals," he explained, "means defining objectives that are Specific, Measurable, Achievable, Relevant, and Time-bound. Leaders must break down their long-term aspirations into smaller, actionable steps that are concrete, quantifiable, and aligned with their vision and values."

Richard Shaw, the head of sales, nodded in agreement. "How can we ensure that our goals are achievable and realistic?"

"Ensuring goal achievability," Jim replied, "involves assessing your resources, capabilities, and constraints to ensure that your goals are within reach and feasible given your circumstances. Leaders must be willing to challenge themselves and step out of their comfort zones, but also recognize the importance of setting goals that are attainable and realistic."

He continued to discuss the importance of setting SMART goals.

"As executives," Jim concluded, "setting personal goals and milestones is essential for guiding our journey towards success and fulfillment. By clarifying our vision, setting SMART goals, and taking consistent action towards their achievement, we can unlock our full potential and create lives that are meaningful, purposeful, and rewarding."

After Jim's presentation concluded, the room buzzed with discussion as the team members analyzed the key strategies for setting personal goals and milestones and shared their own experiences and insights. They now had a clearer understanding of how to define their objectives and take actionable steps towards their achievement, and were motivated to set ambitious yet achievable goals with renewed focus and determination.

As the meeting adjourned, Jim felt a sense of empowerment. With a solid commitment to setting personal goals and milestones, he knew that he and his team were well-equipped to navigate the complexities of leadership with clarity, purpose, and resilience.

About the Author

Goodson Mumba is a multifaceted individual known for his diverse expertise and prolific contributions across various fields. As an infopreneur, Management Consultant, thought leader, and spiritual leader, he has inspired countless individuals through his insightful teachings and impactful writings. Mumba is also an accomplished author, with several notable works to his name, including "Understanding Corporate Worship," "The Years I Spent in a Week," "Management By Harmony," "The CEO's Diary," "Change to Change" and "Creative Thinking for results" His literary works span topics ranging from business management to personal development and spirituality, reflecting his broad range of interests and insights.

With a Master of Business Leadership (MBL) and a Bachelor of Arts in Theology (BTh), Mumba brings a unique blend of business acumen and spiritual wisdom to his work. His educational background is further enriched by a Group Diploma in Management Studies, providing him with a solid foundation in organizational dynamics and leadership principles. Additionally, Mumba holds diplomas in Education Psychology, Leadership and Management Styles, Organizational Behaviour, Financial Accounting, Economic Growth and Development, and Project Management, showcasing his commitment to continuous learning and professional development.

Mumba's expertise extends beyond traditional academic disciplines, encompassing areas such as Neuro-Linguistic Programming (NLP) and Positive Psychology. His diverse skill set is complemented by a range of certifications, including Creative Problem Solving and Decision Making, Life Coaching Fundamentals and Techniques, Professional Life Coaching, and Performance Management System Design. These certifications reflect Mumba's dedication to equipping himself with the tools and knowledge necessary to empower others and drive positive change.

As an author, Mumba's writings reflect his deep understanding of human nature, organizational dynamics, and spiritual principles. His works offer practical insights, actionable strategies, and inspirational guidance for individuals seeking personal growth, professional success, and spiritual fulfillment. Mumba's holistic approach to life and leadership resonates with readers worldwide, making him a respected figure in both the business and spiritual communities.

Overall, Goodson Mumba's diverse background, extensive knowledge, and profound insights make him a sought-after speaker, mentor, and author. His commitment to excellence, lifelong learning, and service to others continues to inspire individuals to unlock their full potential and lead lives of purpose and significance.

Goodson Mumba is renowned for initiating the concept

of Management by Harmony, revolutionizing traditional management practices with a focus on balanced and holistic approaches. He has authored two influential books on this subject: "Introduction to Management by Harmony" and its sequel, "Management by Harmony."

Mumba's work has significantly impacted the field, offering innovative strategies for fostering organizational harmony and efficiency. His contributions continue to shape contemporary management theories and practices.